Dear Animated Bust

Dear Animated Bust

LETTERS TO LADY JULIET DUFF
FRANCE 1915–1918

Maurice Baring

WITH AN INTRODUCTION BY
MARGARET FITZHERBERT

MICHAEL RUSSELL

First published in Great Britain 1981
by Michael Russell (Publishing) Ltd
The Chantry, Wilton, Salisbury, Wiltshire

© Literary estate of the late Maurice Baring 1981

Printed and bound in Great Britain
by Biddles Ltd., Guildford, Surrey

ISBN 0 85955 086 9

Publisher's Note

The appearance of the text calls for explanation. Maurice Baring's wartime letters to Lady Juliet Duff were set up in type at the end of the First World War, faithfully incorporating, it seems, all the idiosyncrasies of spelling, punctuation and general presentation. As if this were not enough, they were reproduced in galley proof of uneven inking and often with some bowing of the lines of type. As far as publication was concerned, there the matter rested. Three sets of the galley proofs were made up into volume form—one for Lady Juliet, one for Maurice Baring and one for Hilaire Belloc. Baring drew on the letters in *Flying Corps Headquarters 1914–1918*, citing always 'from a letter' as his source. Lady Juliet's name did not feature as the recipient, nor was she mentioned in the index. Each letter was edited and its oddities of presentation excised. We have not necessarily avoided passages included in *Flying Corps Headquarters*, because Royal Flying Corps life is obviously central to the context. (There is also a perverse enjoyment, denied to readers of the original book, in considering just how little those snippets about epicyclic gearing and the Acland deflector must have meant to Lady Juliet.) But it must be acknowledged that about an eighth of this book has already appeared in print, albeit in somewhat tidier form. On this occasion we have made use of the original setting but patched it judiciously—keeping the eccentricity, which seems an essential ingredient, but greatly reducing the errors and omissions, which otherwise become, in such profusion, a positive irritation to the reader. Of the original corpus of letters, perhaps a third has been retained. The index, in default of footnotes, will give assistance in identifying *dramatis personae*.

We should like to record our thanks to Lady Maclean for her bravado and patience in entrusting the material to us; to Lady Diana Cooper for making available the silhouette featured on the jacket; to John Saumarez Smith for his usual encouragement and good advice; to Robert Heber-Percy for drawing our attention to the rhyme with which Margaret Fitzherbert concludes her introduction; and to Lady Dorothy Lygon for her editorial help.

Introduction

Maurice Baring was already forty when the First World War began. He did not belong to that endlessly extolled, doomed, 'golden' generation, nor yet to the generation of their parents. He was neither 'soul' nor 'slip', but fell between the two and mixed naturally with both, a ubiquitous and cherished figure in the memoirs of the period. Born in 1874, the eighth of ten children of the first Lord Revelstoke, he was brought up in a privileged, talented, highly educated circle. His childhood was cloudlessly happy: his jokes and culture were rooted in those days of fraulein and mademoiselle and teasing brothers and sisters, and something of that youthful simplicity and humour never left him. He remained unmarried, and at the end of his life, by then a victim of Parkinson's Disease, went to live with Lady Lovat and her children at Beaufort Castle in Invernessshire. He died in 1945.

His literary reputation flourished after the First World War, although his popularity as a novelist was always greater in France than in England. He was a distinguished translator of Russian, French, German and Italian, and a perceptive critic of literature, drama and music. He had not, however, been originally directed towards a life of letters. After Eton and Cambridge, he had been put down for the Diplomatic Service, to which he seemed admirably suited. But his entrance into this career was long delayed by an inability to pass simple examinations in geography and arithmetic. In 1898 two terms spent unofficially at Oxford brought him into contact with a younger Balliol fellowship, which gathered round his two most intimate Oxford friends, Bron Herbert (later Lord Lucas) and Raymond Asquith; while Hilaire Belloc, Baring's senior by four years, became also a close friend. Baring's conversion to Roman Catholicism in 1909 brought him still closer to Belloc. They wrote to each other regularly over the years, frequently in verse:

Dear Maurice,
You write better than Horace;
For you at your worst write madly,
Whereas he at his worst wrote badly.
But neither of us
Writes as well as Theocritus.

Baring joined up in the first few days of the war. Although
he had no military training or background, he happened to
be a friend of Sir David Henderson, Director of Military
Training at the War Office. Henderson was put in charge
of the newly formed Royal Flying Corps and agreed to take
on Baring as an intelligence officer. The result was that Baring
arrived out in France on 12 August 1914, ahead of most of
the regular army and ahead of all the amateurs. While
Henderson was in command, Baring's job was safe and he
soon made himself indispensable. He mastered not only the
jargon of aviation, which he was able to translate into French,
but he actually understood the use and value of each nut
and bolt.

When Henderson returned to London and Trenchard took
over the command of the R.F.C. in France, the outlook
changed. Trenchard already knew Baring from an earlier visit
to France. Baring had been delegated to meet Trenchard and
get him to Headquarters, but the old problem with geography
caused them to strike north from Boulogne, instead of east to
St. Omer. 'A certain intuition', Baring wrote in *Flying Corps
Headquarters 1914–1918*, 'warned me after a time that we were
going the wrong way.' Trenchard, when he arrived to take
command in August 1915, had not forgotten the incident and
intended to sack Baring, whose unmilitary manner and artistic
tastes did nothing to dispel Trenchard's prejudice. He was
put on one month's probation. 'I felt adrift, like a stranded
bondsman face to face with a new Pharaoh, and a bondsman
who felt he had no qualifications.' Happily, in the end,
Trenchard kept him on and later wrote that Baring 'was almost
my second sight in all the difficult tasks that came... He
knew more about what really mattered in war—how to deal
with human nature, how to stir up those who wanted stirring,
how to damp down those who were too excitable, how to
encourage those who were in need of it—than any man I ever
knew.'

Baring's correspondence with Lady Juliet Duff thus flowered in the interstices of a busy, difficult and sometimes dangerous life at the Front. She was not an obviously appropriate recipient for epistolary fireworks. Neither an intellectual nor a Catholic, she was not even clever or well-educated. It was just as well that Baring affected a profound dislike for clever women, although she hid her ignorance quite amiably behind a wall of vagueness. Nor was she accounted much of a beauty by her contemporaries, though both Baring and Belloc thought her lovely. Her gift was that of sympathy; she was a good listener.

Born in 1881, she was the only child of the fourth Earl of Lonsdale. After Lord Lonsdale's death her mother, a Pembroke Herbert whom the Prince of Wales once described as 'a professional beauty', married Lord de Grey, later second Marquess of Ripon. Lady Juliet married Sir Robin Duff in 1903. He was killed in action in October 1914. In 1919 she married Major Keith Trevor, but the marriage ended in divorce in 1926. A rhyme from Maurice Baring survives:

> I've written plenty enough
> To Juliet Duff;
> I'll write nothing whatever
> To Juliet Trevor.

MARGARET FITZHERBERT

H.Q.R.F.C.
13.12.15.

Fleur de mon ame,

The news is that I have been made a Captain. It has
appeared in the Gazette so now you can direct Captain Baring
to me. The second piece of news is that it has cleared up.
The sun shone today for the first time for a month. It was
likewise very cold. The third piece of news is that the man
who puts the muffler on the manifold has arrived and put it on
the manifold. Shortly afterwards the machine was wrecked.
So the result of the experiment is not yet known. I am in the
middle of a game of chess but it takes my adversary twenty
minutes to move so I have time to write to you between the
moves. I am longing to hear from you again. I have not heard
from you since yesterday. You will admit that that is a very
long time to wait. I have asked my sister to buy me a cruet-
stand as a Xmas present for some one else. I have told her
it must not be an artnouveau cruet or a futurist cruet or a
Fortuni cruet or a Fabergé cruet or a Lalique cruet or a Serre
cruet or a Cartier cruet or a Sem cruet or a Max Beerbohm cruet
or a Mestrovic cruet or a Preraphaelite cruet still less a
Pamela Glenconner cruet or an Arthur Ellis cruet or
an Arthur Rackham cruet or a Dulac cruet or an
Arnold Bennett cruet but a solid cruet, possibly a second-hand
cruet, a dignified cruet, a male cruet, a Monsieur cruet and yet
a peace and not a war cruet and not a Parkins and Gotto cruet
still less a Gamage cruet or a Harrods cruet ; an Oxford cruet
rather than a Cambridge cruet, a Cambridge rather than a Har-
vard cruet, and 18th century rather than a 20th century cruet, a
Belloc rather than an Arnold Bennett cruet, a Tory rather than
a Liberal cruet but a Whig rather than a Conservative cruet,
a silver rather than a gold cruet, not a Madame de Beran cruet,
still less a Madame Greyfulle cruet, an English and not a Celtic

1

cruet a London and not a provincial or suburban cruet a mil
huit cent-trente rather than an Mid-Victorian cruet and an
early Victorian RATHER THAN AN empire cruet. Do you
think she will understand?

M.B.

Head Quarters
Royal Flying Corps,

14.12.15.

Chere Zo,

    The post is again interrupted so I suppose we shant get
any letters today. It is Hellish. We had luncheon today with
Philip's A.D.C. General Rawlinson. Philip is very good to
him and very pleased with the way Rawlinson is doing.

    The other news is that there is a Concert tonight at 6 P.M.

    The other news is that there is a spring cleaning in the
office tomorrow.

    The other news is that the King of France arrives here
tomorrow. He is bringing with him Le Fleur de Lys.

    I am also most anxious to hear how you are and whether
Hillary has recovered. He wrote to me saying he was seriously
ill.

    Is that true?

    Have you seen Nan lately?

    Chère Princesse, Je vous souhaite le bon soir.

    Très tendre, très douce, et très belle,
Je suis de vous,
L'esclave très fidèle, très humble et
très loyal,
M.

Head Quarters
Royal Flying Corps,

17 12 15.

Dear Rose Tremière,

    It is a perfectly foul day with bits of drizzling rain.
Osborn arrived yesterday and is now in charge at Head Quarters
which is a great comfort. Please send him a nice Xmas present.

2

Is Macphee still in the hospital? What was your Concert like? I saw all the Queens went to it. and all the soldiers. I cannot sleep at nights for the damp. It penetrates into my bones and gives me feverish tremors.

Do have Maurice mended. I miss him dreadfully.

He is not difficult to mend. I think you ought to have a spare Maurice perhaps a French one called Maurice Ephrussi or Jimmy Rothschild. Which would you rather be?

Shall I give you one for Xmas?

Ade. ave Vale mi Carin.

Tu Mauri

Christmas Day   Head Quarters
                                   Royal Flying Corps,

Chere fraise des bois,

I got two little letters from you last night, one written on a new typewriter which does not write so well as Maurice. We have our Christmas dinner tonight. A turkey shall be eaten. Osborn is very well and is making the house spotlessly clean which is some feat.

I went to Mass this morning and prayed for Juliet.

I wish I had a Christmas present for you but I havent.

The weather is warm and wet and rainy with scudding clouds and drifting gusts of rain and fitful gleams of sun.

Give my best love and the necessary Seasonable wishes to the peoples in the hospital,

                                 Jesuis, Madame,
                                   Ton Ton-Ton.

January 1 1916.   Head Quarters,
                                   Royal Flying Corps,

Chere Jumelle,

Eddy Marsh writes to say the measurements have been made which fills my heart with joy although I have not yet got them. I wish you a happy New Year. I returned from Italy last night. It was, my very dear, one of the most exhausting journeys I have ever done. We motored all day to

Paris then after a hurried dinner we rushed to the Gare de Lyons and thence rushed to Turin. Then the next morning we got up at five and went by train changing five times till the train stopped altogether. Then we hired a motor and drove across the Ticino and for all I know the Rubicon and the Tiber and Lake Maggiore through Lombarda and Novara and Arona to Gallerata where the Italians learn how to fly.

There we inspected the Caproni machine in a shed and thence we drove to Malpensa, where Dante was born and Virgil died, and there we were introduced to forty-five Flying Officers who each one said his name and use and clicked his heels. Then we had luncheon. At the end of luncheon the Captain in command made a speech about delicious England and adorable English people and I made a speech about divine Italians. Then an Italian pilot myself and the man with me went up in the Caproni into the sky. Into the grey misty, sunless, lampless, sullen, unpeopled sky. And as the machine climbed, the curtains of Heaven were rent asunder, and through and over oceans of mist and rolling clouds, naked, majestic, white, shining and glorious rose the Alps, like a barrier; and at our feet dark, as a raven's wing, loomed the waves of Lake Maggiore, fringed with foaming breakers; and the earth was outspread beneath XXXXXXXXXX us like a brown and purple carpet. And we climbed and banked, and banked and climbed and far beneath us a little Maurice Farman fluttered like a white dove. Then suddenly the three engines stopped buzzing and we turned and banked and turned and banked and dived and turned sheer and steep till we gently rolled on to the ground.

Then we spent a few hours in technical conversation and then we went by train to Milan and dined. After dinner we nearly missed the train and finally got back to Turin at midnight. The next day we started for Paris.

A Frenchman sitting next to us in the train whom I knew said to me "Il y a seulement 14 personnes qui voyagent maintenant et on est sur de les rencontre tous. Vous etes un des 14." Castelnau was likewise one of the quatorze.

We reached Paris the next morning and thence hither in the fastest motor in the world.

Au revoir, ma libellule,
Ton Zo-Zou-Zimimini.

January 3 1916.   Head Quarters,
                                   Royal Flying Corps,
Chere Anisette,
    This afternoon while I was out with the General the bomb-store which was crammed with explosives caught fire.
    An officer saw the smoke and went with one corporal, broke into it from the outside and put it out.   Some of the small incendiary bombs were already alight.   I do hope that Maurice will soon be mended.   I miss him terribly.
    Philip Sassoon dined here last night. He is going to London to vote for or against conscription as his conscience will dictate after hearing reasonable arguments on the subject on both sides of the House of Commons.
    As the army is already as big as can be managed and bigger than can be afforded it doesnt make much difference what happens in the matter.   Osborn is very well.   He is a treasure.
    Write to me frequently and at length.   By the way the post has just come and brought me not one letter from you.
                    Fie, Fi-Fi,
                        Votre Bi-bi-le-nou-nou.

                    To Juliet.
    I fondly foolish loved a fool too fair,
    Her folly kept my folly from me, fond,
    Bankrupt I pleaded freedom from the bond,
    Alas she would not cancel it nor tear,
    Nay, but she sealed it with her silken hair
    Enchanting with the spice of Trebizond,
    Nay, but she struck me with a magic wand,
    And dazzled me with aromatic air.
    O golden Hermes, why dost thou delay?
    Have pity on my heavy melancholy,
    Come with the South wind and the flowers of May,
    And from the grasses pluck a root of moly ;
    Then will the foolish witch I thought divine,
    Run screaming in a rout of silly swine.
Do you think this poem is rude enough? I fear not.
will try and write a better and a ruder one tomorrow.
                    yours M B.

5

Head Quarters,   Royal Flying Corps,
26. 1. 16.
Tres chere ZOU ZOU,
        The smells in the house this morning are appalling.
A bottle of paraffin which was used against all orders to light
the fire was upset on the office carpet besides this there is a
strong smell of beastly soap and a stale smell of sheets besides
this there are whiffs of cooking and a smell of rancid oil.
        The result is I feel sick.
        I forgot to mention there is also a smell of Three Castles
cigarette and third class railway carriage.
        I will soon write to you in verse in the Georgian style.
A sonnet beginning
                I was a bloody fool to love you Dear
                A bloody fool to love a fool like you,
                O foolish fair, o fondest foul untrue.
                        &&&&&&&&
                                Yrs
                                        Cabuchon.

29.1.16.   H.Q. R.F.C. B.E.F.
                                                        France.
Chere Zo,
        Thank you for letter. I think I told you it was all right
about O.   Also that the cigars are very good indeed.   Raymond
Asquith dined here last night.   This morning I saw Philip.
        Is Maurice mended yet? If you want it mended quickly
you should take it to the makers in the Strand and not to
Harrods.
        I hope he will be mended soon. I miss him very much.
                        Hi Hi ton
                                Ti-ti.

Head Quarters
Royal Flying Corps,   January 30. 1916.
Chere Libellule,
        Postal communication with England being for the

moment interrupted I receive no letters and doubt whether this will reach you for some time.

Nevertheless I write not as I will but as I must like the linnet.

There is a dense fog. I trust the Zeppelin that went to Paris last night got caught in it.

Yours in hope,
Rouetabille.

H.Q. R.F.C.   31.1.16.

Chere Pointe d'Asperge,

I know exactly what has happened to Maurice. They have changed him and sent you one with another type. Namely the standard type. They make them in four types.

It may interest you to know that rotary engines are being made in England.

The Caproni has stationary engines.

The point about an engine is not whether it is rotary or stationary but whether it is a *good* stationary engine or a XXXX *bad* stationary engine, a *good* rotary engine or a *bad* rotary engine a *fast* rotary engine or a *slow* rotary engine. Both types exist.

Bon Soir, Charmante Hortense,
Ton
Louis Philippe.

2. 2. 16.

Head Quarters, Royal Flying Corps, B E F, France.

Chere Perce-Neige,

A Zeppelin at night is the German's delight.

A Zeppelin at morning is the German's warning.

It froze in the night, But it thawed in the morning,
(It didnt)

The ground is a sight! It thawed I mean froze in the night.

The Zeppelin's delight is to bomb without warning.

It froze in the night but it thawed in the morning.

I feel sick. The Huns make me tired when they say they bombarded the fortress of Montmartre as a retaliation for the air attack on the open town of Freiburg which was itself an answer to the bombardment of about sixteen villages at Epernay. This bombardment being evidently a trial trip for Paris. The stupid owls make me tired and sick. I dined out last night. The dinner was good and the wine was still better I say it who should, the dinner was good, there was port from the wood and a mango from Quetta the dinner was good and the wine was still better.

!Hi ja de la Belleza !
Adios,
Macro.

Candlemass. 1916.   H.Q. R.F.C. France.
Chere Girofla,
        A was the Avro that fell in the soup
        B was the Bristol that climbed on the loop,
        C was the Curtis that went for a Zep,
        D was a delicate dangerous Dep
        E was for Essen the home of the Guns
        F was the Fokker the pride of the Huns.
        G was for Garros interned near the Spree
        H was for Hawker who got the V.C.
        I was for Immelmann somewhere in Heaven,
        J was a Joyride from Dover to Devon &&&&&&&
                &&&&&&&&&&&&&&
                Yrs,
                    M.B.

Head Quarters,   Royal Flying Corps,
February 3 1916.
Charmante Doremi,
        I have just come back from a long day's outing. I hasten to write to you and to inform you that I do not believe the heir apparent of the Sultan died a natural death! I believe shall I say it? that he was murdered?

8

MURDERED. Most foully murdered !
    Juliet, her name was Juliet, she was tall,
    Tall as the stem of some high tropic flower,
    That lights the darkness for one golden hour,
    Then lets its bright unfaded petals fall,
    So that the spring may have a shining pall,
    So that the fairies may not lack a bower,
    When comes the swift remorseless Summer shower,
    And all the leaves with rain are musical.
    Her eyes were softer than a plumage rare,
    Where hues of dawn and twilight mingled are ;
    Her eyes were brighter than a single star
    Alone in the broad morning's azure air,
    Or like large stars reflected in a pool,
    So lustrous were her eyes, so soft, so cool.
    I have just got two letters from you. It is very easy to
write bad verse on a typewriter. If you will dabble in black
magic of course you will get unlucky cards. I very much
deprecate the practice of dabbling in black magic. I think one
is instantly punished for it. Almost on the same day. God
cannot tolerate it.
                    I am yrs
                            Le chevalier des brouillards.

        6.2.16.
Dear Poule aux yeux d'Or,
    I will write no more as by the time I shall be in England
you will be getting this. I mean the other way round.
    Au revoir un long au revoir. Comme un long sanglot tout
chargé d'au revoir.
                    Yours,
                        Jean Christophe.

H.Q. R.F.C. 18.2.16.
Chere Jujube,
    I went to the Boatswains Mate and enjoyed it. The
beginning ought to be cut and it all ought to be played

or with a very short interval and without that grotesquely *a coté* scenery which would do very well for a mystery by Andreev or a fairy morality by Maeterlinck but which is simply *silly* for a Jacobs story and kills the production besides making acting and singing impossible and giving the audience in the stalls stiff necks.

Let me know whether you got rid of your house and what happened about it.

I am going to Paree tomorrow.

Amen.,

Yrs M B.

H Q R F C B E F,
24.2.16.
Spirto Gentil,

I came back from Paris yesterday where I spent a day with T. It was rather fun. The Zeppelin was announced for 9 30 but it was shot on the way and brought down to the huge delight of everybody.

It is colder than Hell today so cold I cant manage the Capital letters. Do you find the same difficulty in the cold weather? I believe Hillary is still in France?

The pilot whose leg was blow up by an Archie the day before yesterday after bringing his observer safely down had it cut off with a pair of scissors!

Yours&
Boubaki.

H Q R F C 27.2.16.
Chere Madame Pinson,

Can you send me one readable book of any kind. The longer the better ?????????

It is thawing. I would that I was too.

Yrs

George (Alexander not Rex)
P.S.

Triste sonant, fractaeque agitata crepuscula silvae.

Blighty.

I want to go to Blighty, for I do
Love Blighty more than any foreign land ;
I want to see the shingle and the sand,
And Battersea, Vauxhall and Waterloo.
I want to hear the noises of the Strand ;
Through the red fog I want to see a barge
Move slowly down the river looming large ;
I want to hear the music of the band.
I want to see the children at their play,
Feeding the ducks upon the Serpentine ;
I want to hear the barrel-organs bray,
When the wet sunset in a narrow mews
Reflected, makes the pavement puddles shine,
And ragamuffins yell the racing news.

H.Q. R.F.C.   2.3.16.
Chere Yolande,
    O roucoulante extase de la tour abolie, how are you?
Ther was a slight frost here last night.
And now that Henry James is dead
There's very little to be said.
How is Hillary?
A British pilot shot a German Albatross yesterday with his crossbow.

The German was so sure of being shot down that he had brought his luggage with him which consisted of a schnurbartbinde and a small dolls portmanteau.

The Saxons are fed up with the war. How different from the Anglos !

               Yours ever
                   El Desdichado.

H.Q.R.F.C. 8.3.16.
O Liebig mein, cher extrait,
    It snowed all day yesterday and today the ground is white as snow.

I am covered with blains.

Thank you for sending me the book. I liked the one about the Millionaire you sent from Sotherans. The other one defeated me.

Raymond dined here last night.

Phip was to have and chucked. We have got a nice Frenchman in the house who is liaison officer for aviation called Ferriere.

Wasnt it terrible about Desmond FitzGerald? He was such an angel.

Today Lent begins. I wonder if Hillary begins his water-waggon stunt?

It is very trying for everybody else.

Do you still go out in Liberal circles?

We have got a new machine. It did its trials yesty. day before. It is a great deal faster than the Fokker.

It climbs like lightning. (YPP 6000 feet in two minutes)

Yours &

Bouillabaisse.

H.Q. R.F.C.   12.3.16.

My Dear Ju

The Hispano-Suiza did 90 on the Pitot with the cut down propeller.

I hope the Le'Vasseur Nieuport propeller will arrive to morrow.

They say the engine with the silencer is faster. This is difficult to believe. But I do believe it.

She missed badly as Bettington was flying across so he had to shut off.

The fan in the acetone dope room is out of order so they were told to knock off work there.

In future no Raf signalling lamps are to be kept in the 2nd A P.

The doping room there was not satisfactory. They were repairing a plane there which is against orders as it was laid down that *only doping* is to be done there.

In the M T they were making water trailers for the Wings. Unnecessary! M.B.

15.3.16.   H.Q.
                                    R.F.C. B.E.F.
My Dear Lady A——,
        There has been no post for two days so I dont know
whether I have got any letters or not.   The Spring has arrived,
and with it a number of birds.
        I wish all of our friends wrote on a typewriter dont you?
Some do but then they dont write themselves which is not the
same thing.
        I have nothing to say.   You know my views on Life.   You
know my views on War.   You know my views on *the* war.
You know my views on the Deflector Propeller.
        Today the Hispano got the legs of the Martinsyde with the
Lang Propeller.
        The Le Vasseur propeller absorbs the power but not the
efficiency and with it the Hispano on the B E beats the Bristol
on the climb but not on speed.
        The Pitot tube not having been calibrated it was not
reliable.
        I am tired of tears and laughter.
        An L.V.G. and an Aviatik and an Albatross have all found
a happy home in our lines.
                        I am
                        Chere Mees,
                        Your
                        Bellac.
                        (Not Belloc)

17.3.16.
Donna Immobile ou Dame Immeuble,
        Your letter about the dinner made me scream with
laughter.   Dinner in Lent with Hillary is always a trouble.
        Tell him that while the Church orders and organises a
certain abstinence and certain fasts, to make a stunt of one's
own to drink wine is a Protestant even an Anabaptist idea.
The Church especially lays down that Vinum jejunum non
fregit Wine does not break fast.   I didnt see anything on
outside.
                        Yrs M.

                        13

St . Patrick's   H.Q.R.F.C.
    Day.   B.E.F.
1916.
Dear Lady Egerton of Tatton,
    Thank you so very much for your most interesting
letters.
    I hear Hillary has begun his Lenten abstinence from wine.
It is a very severe penance for his friends. But I dont think
one ought to discourage it.
    Personally I am more than thankful when that season draws
to a close.
    How did your dinner with Evan and H go off?
    I have had nothing decent to smoke for 6 weeks.
    In the back gunmounting of the Morane Biplane in A
flight of No 1 the taper-peg of the gas-regulator had no packing.
    Also the shock-absorber on the drum of the Lewis gun
which is round was being changed for a flat and weak one ; if
this turns out to be reasonable the change must be adopted
generally. No 7 still paint their tailplanes ! which is unnecessary and makes the machine heavier.
                            Yrs M B.

24 March, 1916.
H Q R F C B E F France.
    My Dear Liane de Pougy,
    I think it quite extraordinarily kind of you to send me those
excellent cigarettes and those beautiful cigars. I have just
come back from Paris. Where Morane was told he was making
the nonsense which he had been doing badly. I had to do the
telling and I nearly laughed in translating T's fiery and astound-
ingly direct criticism and appreciations. At dinner the fish
was high, the ham undercooked, the cold chicken tasted of
train. The waiter broke the plates. In fact a war dinner.
(upstairs) (at the Ritz.) I thought of Hillary and laughed.
    I also saw Monsieur Nieuport and Monsieur Saulnier and
the (Nieuport) Single-seater (Hispano-Suiza). Also the Acland
gunmounting ; when the gun was fired the cartridges came out
intact the wrong end and hit one in the face. This was a pity.

It was very cold in Paris. It is still very cold here. I hope the war will be over soon. My Haircutter told me you were expected at the Riviera. He also told me that you didnt like — — as much as you used to do but that you thought his wife was nice. So I gather he knows you very well.

Yrs Destournelle.

Head Quarters, 26.3.16.
Royal Flying Corps, B.E.F., France
Dear Mrs. De Vere Stackpole,
I wrote to you last night but before the letter went I threw it in the fire as it contained a cheque for £23.
It is still very windy and cold.
The night before last I was woken up three times by the cold and once by a mouse. I got up early and when I walked into the dismal dining room the Adjutant who was sitting there eating a fried egg said :
'' On a day like this ones glad to be alive.''
These sentiments happened to be the opposite of mine.
Which would you rather not or rather if obliged which would you chose to escape death
to dress for ever like — —
to have — — to stay with you forever and never missing a meal
To have a very slightly blue nose.
I told you many things in the letter I threw away but cannot now remember one of them.
I am Madam,
Your devoted,
Aubrey Tanqueray.

Head Quarters, 28.3.16.
Royal Flying Corps, B.E.F., France.
My Dear Mrs. Wooland,
owing to the Prime Minister the german submarines and the bad weather we have received no post for days with the exception of what arrived par la voie des airs.

The cold is indescribable. It is windy cutting gusty cloudy and raw. Notice that having said it was indescribable I at once proceeded to describe it. This is a well known trick of pulpit preachers who say the story of the Prodigal Son is too well known to repeat "we all know" . . . they then proceed to repeat and expand it at length . . . in their own words . . .

I have no doubt I shall receive many letters from you as soon as a post does arrive. We are moving into another chateau. Osborn is arranging the demanagement and the emanagement. He is thoroughly enjoying it. I am not. Somebody says suddenly what about extra sheets and a leaf for the dining-room table? And I turn pale with rage. However I have learnt to be patient. My XXXX spirit is broken. And never again serenely in the sunshine as before shall I air my úbris. You dont know what that means. Hillary will tell you. The new chateau is beautiful. You had better buy it after the war.

How is Nan?

An air professor, Professor Lanchester not Lancaster, is staying in the house. When I told him last night at 11 P.M. his bed was out of doors and a long way off in the dark and rain he cried.

Yrs M. B.

H Q R F C
31 3 16.
Chère Madame Rouff,

Our move is over and we are living in a vast chateau about three hundred years old once a XXXXXXXXX Bishops House. Damaged but not destroyed in the French Revolution with huge thick walls.

I am too melancholy to write. I feel the burden and the heavy weight of all this unintelligible war. Also I hate having luncheon in a motor and I always have loathed sandwiches they remind me of children being sick in the train (Great Western).

So I underfed and overworried, and the cook is very tiresome.

Write to me

Arsène Houssaye.

HQ. R.F.C.
     1.4.16.
Avril este de retour la saison des roses de ses levres mi-
closes sourit a la tout autour,
     Helas J'ai dans le coeur une tristesse affreuse.
I received your letter last night for which many thanks. No
wonder David looks harried. They make him responsible
for what they refused to do before the war. If it hadnt
been for David we should have had no Flying Corps at all.
Everybody is harried. and worried to death. I think the Mergs
ought to give Billing an iron cross. He is doing them a real
service.
     Nett result of air agitation so far
A. Positive. Not the hastening of one bolt wire turnbuckle
     or cable.
B. Negative.
     1. The dislocation of the administration in England and
France.
     2. Hindering of operations in France.
     3. Danger of spreading alarm and despondency among the
younger personnel.
     However I went to 8 squadrons yesterday and all the pilots
foamed at the mouth when Billing was mentioned. and said
he ought to be hanged.
     Only you can imagine this kind of thing doesnt cheer them
up.
     Write often.
               Yrs M B.

     2. 4. 16.
Douce,
     The intelligentsia are the same all the world over. I feel
for them an elemental hatred.
     Our French interpreter asked if he might bring a friend
to dinner who was a doctor at the French hospital.
     He came. He was in peace time an inhabitant of
Armentières. He said he wanted to see an English Mess. He
evidently thought the English were wild beasts.

17

Before tasting any dish he shouted to the interpreter
    Qu'est que c'est que cette soupe?
    Qu'est que c'est que ce poisson?
As the dishes were purely French cooked by a Frenchman there was nothing very odd about them.

So when he asked this the third time I had the great satisfaction of saying :
    "C'est un plat qui s'appelle poulet roti."
There wasnt even any bread sauce to make it odd.

He was just like XXXXXXXXXXXXXXXXXX any kind of "Intelligent." At the end of dinner he said "mais les cigares sont tout a fait bons." (They were those you had sent!) I said "Je vous crois Monsieur" I then said that if he would permit me I would send him a box. A rash promise. Which I repeated later. Will you send me another box to send him? Send the smallest possible, not more than 10 if possible. It is a great waste. But as I said he was not to think that if there was any delay I had forgotten I suppose I must do it.

Write to me often. Life is so tiring at present that a letter is a great relaxation.

I feel like a man who is engaged with a party of a thousand other men in rolling a huge stone up hill that rolls back like the stone of Sisyphus. Autis epeita pedonde kulindeto laas anaidees.

Hillary will translate. Be very kind to David. His great wisdom is being proved every day. Every thing to which he objected in the past and which was done has been proved wrong and every thing which he advocated and which was done has been proved right.
    Yrs M B.

3.4.16.
Dear Madame Porges,
    Yours to hand many thanks.

It was not very long so this shall be still shorter if possible. Do ut des as Bismarck so wittily remarked when he kicked the Pope on the shin.

The weather is glorious. Write to me a real letter full of news and gossip.

Have you ever tried writing like this on real paper? Its
rather fun.
Send me one gramophone record. A good one. Not
Harry Lauder. Not Vesti la Giubba.

Your Uncle.

Head Quarters,
Royal Flying Corps,   6.4.16.
B.E.F. France.

Suave fanciulla,
Celeste Aida, ebben qual nuovo fremito ritorna vincitor,
un di all'azzuro spázio, di tu sé fidele eri, tu che macchiavi
quell' anima ridente, il cielo, se il mio nome, Testa adorata.
Io no ho che una povera stanzetta, Ah Mimi tu piu. Che
gelida manina! A voi tutti salute, Voi lo sapete. Non più
di fiori su queste rose la ci darem, il cor nel contento. In terra
solo, O Lisbona, una furtiva lagrima da qual di che.
Infelice e tuo credevi, O dei verd' anni miei, vieni meco
sol di rose. Salve dinmora, a tanto amor, XXXXXXXXX
spirito gentil amor ti vieta per viver vicino qui sdegno
invano Alvaro le minaccie. Madre pietosa, Oh tu che
segno agl' angeli solenne in quest'ora non chiuder gli occhi,
vaghi studenti udite cielo e mar; L'amo come il fulgor del
creato pescator affonda l'esca suicidio!
Voce di Donna o d'angelo, Aprila bella la fenestrella, t'eri
un giorno ammalato. A muto asil. Spettro santo, O vecchio
cor Amato, che batti vieni al contento profundo chi mi frena,
cruda funesta. Fra poco a me ricovero spargi d'amaro pianto.
Tu che a Dio spiegasti, Vien, la mia vendetta, O quanti occhi
fissi ora a noi! Un bel di vedremo, disse il saggio, ma tu,
sfiorata Donna, non vidi mai. Bella e di sol vestita, che vuol
dir ciò? Il mio Lionel m'appari tutt' amor solo profugo dai
campi dai prati l'altra notte. Son lo spirito che nega, addio
Mignon, Oh d'amore, Ah bello a me ritorna, casta Diva. Ite
sul colle o Druidi; non piu andrai Voi che sapete ora e per
sempre si per ciel.
Ah! forsè lui Parigi o cara tacea la notte placida perche
tremar?
Ah si ben mio d'amor sull' alli rosee di geloso di quella pira.

19

Malreggendo all'aspro assalto mira d'acerbe lagrime stride la
vampa vivra contende il giubilo,.
 Buona Zaza, del mio buon tempo ora e per sempre,
  Addio, manella mia, XXXXXXX batti, batti,
   O sole mio, ombra mai fu,
    De Tura.

7.4.16.

Bonnie sweet Bessie,
 I send you my best wishes and my kind regards.
General Rawlinson is wearing black field boots. On the other
hand General Birch is wearing buff or beige putties. General
Trenchard is wearing brown field boots. Captain Baring is
wearing gaiters.
  Ever your most obedient,
   Lausbube.

8 4 16.

Lent is drawing to a close and all Hillary's friends are
beginning to breathe. I have found out why Maurice sometimes writes faint. It is nothing to do with the ribbon. It
simply means the machine wants oiling and greasing. I think
the attacks on David Henderson are too dastardly. They will
end by making him go and that will be a disaster. I hate the
newspapers and the politicians. Raymond dines here tonight.
I like him. Not a day passes but that I write to you.
Voce de prima vera,
  Addio,
   yrs Pablo de Sarasate.

12.4.16.

My Dear Priscilla,
  That Italian letter was really very clever. Every
phrase in it was the beginning of a very well known song such
as "Batti Batti." There was no word in it that didnt belong

20

to the beginning of a song and sometimes but not always it made a certain sense just enough and not too much. That was the point. How tiresome to have to explain! In any case it looked sensible enough.

But which would you rather?

XXXXXXXXXXX Have to sleep in a different place every night for the rest of your life.

Have to sleep *every* night of the rest of your life at the Grand Hotel Birmingham? or

Have to go on the stage and to be a mediocre actress and act and act for the rest of your life not well enough to earn the *slightest* praise and not bad enough to be sacked. And never once to have an interesting part?

The weather here is as cold as England today.

I have been much cheered of late by some gramophone records of Reynaldo Hahn.* There is one called Barchetta which is quite delicious.

Recommend it to Bron. He would like it.

I am your faithful advocate,

Paul Mounet. (Artiste de la Comédie Française).

If you swear to me to write everyday I will swear to write everyday. It doesnt matter if the letter only has one comma in it.

"une virgule! O gudule!

O Sainte Ursule,

I recommend you an extraordinary book called

The Spoonfed Anthology.

* A French singer.

Postscript. The French have got a pilot of genius called Navarre. He shot down 4 Mergs in one day on our side of the line the record so far.

This piece of paper is bigger than I thought

Which would you rather have no hot water for the rest of your life either to wash or drink or for hot water bottle.

Live at Wellington New Zealand for ever or stutter so badly that it took you five minutes to say every word.

Yrs,

Maurice de Bunsen

18.4.16.

My Dear Malvernia (Molly)

(Best of British sparkling table waters),
the weather is so foul that I cant write to you in that spirit of
cheerfulness I should like to.

I saw Philip this morning who had seen your mother.

An equinoxial gale is going on. And other signs of "Ce
coquin de Printemps."

When the war is over,
When the fightings done,
When the

When the

When the

Too tired to write this evening 19 April never to be forgotten
Primrose Day. I have translated a whole German brochure
about how to erect the Fokker one French report on Night
reconnaissance and written three long letters in French about
bombsights.

Therefore my head is empty and my typewriter recalcitrant
and in fact I am not going to write another word. Except this
one, namely

MAURICE.

20 April 16.

Chere Bilitis,

Je vous envoie cette lettre afin que votre nom aborde
heureusement aux epoques lointaines, and to tell you that having
snatched a little sleep last night I am a little less tired today.
The General has got an A D C and this puts just ten years back
to my life as it means I no longer have to telephone nor do
the household accounts. It is a load off. I am so haapr. I
am so happy. On the other hand I have far more other things
to do so in spite of being happy I am too fatigued to write to
you. More than this.

Yours M. Bernhardt

22

H.Q.R.F.C.   22.4.16.
Dear Sir,
        very many thanks for yours of yesterday. With regard
to the request made by you and recently reiterated that I should
forward you a cheque for the amount due to you I have to
remind you that bright gold is not the thing that is most rare
in the sad-hoped life of mortals nor do steel nor couches of
silver, XXXXXXXXXXXXXXX, nor the heavy-laden fields,
fruitful in themselves, of the spacious earth, so shine to the
eye as the single-minded spirit of good men.
        Never therefore be tempted to barter virtue for *unjust gain*.
The best thing for a mortal is to have health, and the next
to have been born fair of form, and the third to be rich without
guile, and the fourth to have fun with your friends.
        It is regrettable Sir, that XXXXXXXX none of these con-
ditions are fulfilled in your case.
        My last word therefore shall be that virtue has sure glory,
but wealth is sometimes an appanage of the basest among men.
Please lay all this to heart and dont bother me further with
your so-called account. Remember that war is war and that
necessity knows no law. Recall to mind the pregnant phrase
of the German Minister with regard to a scrap of paper and
never forget that it behoves us to be economical in paper as
well as in red gold or notes of currency.
                        I am Sir, with great truth,
                            Your obedient Servant,
                                (for) M. Diagoras.
                                W. T. Le Phill.
Messrs Moulton & Co,
        Furniture Dealers,
            Great Portland Street,
                London.

                        April 27, 1916.
                MAURICE BARING BORN 1874.
        My Dear Douce-amere,
        to-day is my birthday so I wish you many happy returns of
the day. A spring has broken in Maurice so I have been unable
to write for the last half hour.

                            23

Out of the window in front of the Louis Treize farm, one tree is now completely green. I dont know what kind of tree it is but it is not either a Palm tree or a Upas tree or a Eucalyptus or an ever-green oak or a monkey tree or a Wellingtonia.
The elms on the other hand are still bare.
I recommend to your attention the plays of Paul Claudel. They are extremely beautiful. I recommend *La Jeune fille Volaine* and *L'Echange*.
Raymond Asquith has got a son. He is going to call it Easter Sunday as he was born on Easter Sunday.
I havent written to you for the last two days or the last three days even because I have been as busy as a dog.
Nobody who has not been here knows what a strain it is. Not what you have to do but the feeling of being surrounded by live wires of their being a spark and a shock at any minute about the most different things.
Now you can see Hillary with comfort this Eastertide. We must invent a different mortification for him I think.
The aeroplanes have been splendid lately scattering the Germans and little Patrick brought down an Albatross from fourteen thousand feet after attacking it three times.
The French have driven the Boches out of the air at Verdun.
Navarre is the greatest flying genius the world has ever seen. He makes rings round everybody else and spirals down nose diving. But he has all the faults of a genius and sometimes sulks for a week. He brought down 4 Boches in a hour.

G. Maubant.

Head Quarters,
    Royal Flying Corps, B E F France.   14.5.16.
Dear Melisande,
    I am sending this by Osborn who is going on leave.
    I sent him a cocktail shaker. It cost sixteen shillings being made of pseudosilver.
    I am exceedingly tired after my visit to London where I saw hardly any of my friends.
    Send me back a surprise by Osborn.
                    Yours
            Mas Parnet (Laureat de l'Academie des Sports).

18.5.16.

Douce Violaine,

Thank you for the letter which I received last night. We had three punctures yesterday and finally the last spare tyre came off so we had to walk home. Such is life. The young corn was very green and the partridges were running about in couples and the sky was like those of the post impressionists all lilac and the sun was a blazing red ball and the moon was a tawny round shield.

And the cockchafers buzzed like small Blériots and the B Es buzzed like large cockchafers.

Write and tell Philip you have heard that Canadian troops have been billeted in his house at Hythe or are going to be. It will give him the frousse.

Osborn has had a fearful row with the French cook. I expect it was the cook's fault ; on the other hand I think they are determined to get rid of the cook. If they do they will be *foolish ;* as he is a *good* cook and they will quarrel with any cook at least they always have so far. And if the cook goes the General will think it is Osborn's fault.

As before he came matters never reached such a crisis and the quarrels used only to be mild.

If he talks to you about it make him see reason.

I think the new A D C strafes the cook too much and he the cook then goes and vents his temper in the kitchen.

It is a mistake to strafe Frenchmen, they should be flattered. Otherwise one fine day they fly at you with a knife.

Anabal' anow to geeras,

O kala Juliet.

’Ανάβαλ’ ἄνω τὸ γῆρας,
ὦ καλά.

Raymond has gone back to his regiment.

Yours

Fanfan.

21.5.16.

’Ω καλλιπρόσωπε, χαριτόφωνε, θάλος ἐρώτων, if possible send me a book to read, an amusing book of any kind which I can read in beeds.

25

The weather is wonderful. Ah me! but the *war* is bloody.
Would that we were at peace and would that we two were
Maying.
’Ω γλυκεῖ’ εἰρήνη, πλουτοδότειρα βοτοῖς
χαίρετε   Μαῦρος.

Head Quarters,   22.5.16.
Royal Flying Corps, B. E. F., France.
Princesse enqui le ciel mit un esprit si doux,
I had something very important to tell you and I cant
remember what it was. My bath is ready so I needs must go
and have it. It is the 2nd bath I have had since the war began.
                     Yours Madam, Yours,
                                Xavier de Montepin.

Head Quarters   23.5.16.
Royal Flying Corps, B.E.F., France.
Alma de mi alma, why this silence?
I have been promoted and I am now a Staff Captain and shall
wear in future a red hat, Scarlet tabs and a blue band round my
arm : light blue dark blue and vermilion.
Thank you very much for the cigars which are quite excel-
lent and just what I greatly needed.
It is kind of you to do your bit by me.
                     Your loving,
                                Patrick Campbell.

26.5.16.
     Ariane ma soeur,
     I regret not to have heard from you today nor yesterday
nor the day before nor the day before that. Far be it from me
to complain, knowing what a hard life is yours and how busy.
     I killed a cockchafer last night,
     That soared in spirals round my bed.
     Do you agree that I did right?

26

I killed a cockchafer last night.
It would persist, with all its might,
In buzzing round and round my head.
I killed a cockchafer last night,
That soared in spirals round my head.
A vous Castellane.   M. B.

Head Quarters,
    Royal Flying Corps,   France.
    13.6.16.
Pulcherrima,
        epistolam tuam hodie recepi. Gratias ago. Dies sine
epistola tamquam nox.

I suppose at the Day of Judgment all the actors and
actresses of London will give a star performance in honour of
the event and — — will make a speech and Lady — — will
preside at the tea room and — — and — — will sell the
programmes.

The English people when their religion was taken away
from them had to make a new one.

The Puritans made a strong doleful one but it was too boring
for the populous and too austere so they made something else
namely the adoration of

(a) The royal family instead of God.

(b) The aristocracy instead of the Saints.

(c) Actors and actresses instead of the Blessed and quasi
    Saints or Saints on the way towards canonisation.

So that now — — and — — play the the same part as the
Household Gods did in antiquity whereas Lords and Ladies
Baronets and Knights are as the DemiGods and heroes and
King Queens and Dukes are like the Gods of Olympus.

It continues to be cold.

The General has got a cold in his head but does not admit it.
He did nobble it was a womans voice on the telephone.   He
was quite pleased with the joke.

I am not in a good temper.

I feel as if I was not rigged to standard and I want tuning up.
            Da nie smushchaietsia Sertze vashe,
                                                Oshima.

27

Head Quarters,
Royal Flying Corps.   14.6.16.
Douce Violaine,
       I am sorry about the carbuncle but it might have been
a garnet which would have been worse.
       A carbuncle is very underrated gem.   Be careful with it.
You better let Cartier or Faberge or Boucheron see to it.
       The cold is intense. I am wearing my thickest soks or socks.

When the fish went to war,
and the birds went to sea,
There was no peace more
in the old countree

and the jolly little lollypops that sat upon the sand,
They took to playing cricket and to bowling overhand,

And they all drank tea,
In the down-town store,
When the birds went to sea,
and the fish went to war.

When the fish went to war,
And the birds went to sea,
XXXXXXX They all played Spohr
XXX in Bonny Dundee,

And the jolly little lollypops that sat upon the grass
They gave up picking daisies and they cried " Alas Alas,"

And drinks were free
In the town of Bangalore
When the birds went to sea,
And the fish went to war.
When the fish went to war
And the birds went to sea,
They banged the front door,
In the new rectory,

And the jolly little lollypops that sat upon the ground,
They gave up grinding coffee and danced round and round and
       round,

And they all read " She "
till their eyes were sore,
When the birds went to sea,
And the fish went to war.

28

When the fish went to war,
And the birds went to sea,
They made bricks without straw
In Trincomalee

And the jolly little lollypops that sat upon the chairs
They gave up knitting stockings and they combed their golden
hairs,

And Sir Beerbohm Tree
said "I ll act no more,"
When the birds went to sea,
And the fish went to war.

The domestic situation is quiet. On the kitchen front there is nothing to report and we are still holding Hut No 156.

I am Madam
Your subservient servant,
Elisha Argalles.

Head Quarters,
R F C B E F France.

15.6.16.

Nienagladnaya, moya radost,
I am in receipt of two letters for which I am truly thankful.

I am glad your chin is better. You must be singing like Hillary,
"I'm tired of binding my chin "
The Gates of Heaven are open wide
To let poor Juliet in."

Daylight saving stunt began to day much to the detriment of everybody's temper. Nobody has had quite enough sleep as we went to bed by God's time and got up by Man's time.

Talking of Time dont forget that Love is not Time's fool.
One mouthpiece enclosed.

I am running short of cigarettes. I wonder if you could go to Marcovitch 13 Regent Street for me and ask them to send me two hundred cigarettes of the same tobacco made as that which they supply to Bron, but not with such a short mouthpiece but with a longer one such as the enclosed. The short

one, when moistened, falls off, and the incandescent ash falls
on the the chin or lip, and abraids it and burns it, causing a
blister, carbuncle or garnet.

I believe. I neednt repeat the rest of the creed.

When I am dead waste no salt tears on me,
nor veil your beauty in a garb of woe,
For I should feel your infelicity
&&&&&&&&&&& &&&&&&&&&& &&&&&&&&&&

    Ever your faithful,

        Sotheby, Wilkinson & Hodge.

                       17.6.16.

Chere Douceamere,

    This morning I am unserviceable (with engine) and am
not doing full revs. In fact I am losing speed. But I shall
be all right for school work later on in the day.

The sun is shining but the canteen tooth powder is nasty
and tastes of brick. Will you order me a box from Pope
Roach's of toothpowder. Calvert, British. Pink. Large size.

Hillary's landing articles are very funny. They would
generally be true if all he talked about was a mathematical
proposition and if everybody concerned did every thing they
do for a sensible reason. Unfortunately the unexpected plays
a large part and fortunately also.

I think it would be rather a good thing if he changed the
character of his articles.

Also if he added pictures. I mean a picture of Verdun for
instance by himself. Not a map but a picture.

You can tell him all this from me.

        Your most loving,

            Cadet Roussel.

                June 18. 1916.

          Battle of Waterloo fought 1815.

Dear Lady DeRos,

    Thank you very much for your two most important
letters.

The *Cigarette Question.*

The same sample mouthpiece which I enclosed and which I enclose again today so as to avoid all possible error and confusion is not, believe me, the same sized mouthpiece as that mouthed by Lord Lucas.

That mouthed by Lord Lucas is shorter so much shorter that is just too short, and when moistened, as I said before, the cigarette loses flying speed, then stability, sideslips and crashes on to the chin where it engenders a festering carbuncle.

If Marconivitch says he cant make a mouthpiece as large and as long that is to say *as long* (as the width is of no consequence) as that in the sample ask him why the Hebrew Lipkin of 33 Tottenham road can?

The Hebrew Lipkin of 33 Tottenham Road was discovered by Countess Benck. And his shape of cigarette is quite satisfactory but ' I find ' the tobacco he puts inside the cigarettes is unsmokeable. If Marconivitch cant do this I will have none of his cigarettes.

All sensible cigarettemakers buy these cartridges or as the Russians call them *Gilzi* ready made. (And fill them with tobacco by means of a small wood contrivance.)

Couldnt Marconi find out where the Hebrew Lipkin buys his Gilzi?

Second Important Question.

Juliet wants a new ribbon. But such is her extreme fastidiousness that only one sort will satisfy her and that is called Black and Red Record Pigeon Brand Standard Type writer Co Croton U S A and can be bought near the Hotel Cecil or at Harrods.

I strongly advise you to feed Maurice with new ribbons often. Do not stint him. His whole demeanour depends on this.

Third Most Important Question.

I want a light box in which to put cigarettes it can be made of anything except porphyry, alabaster, Greek-glass, Lapis-Lazuli, platinum, tortoiseshell or mother of pearl.

It must be 6 inches by three and a half by two. In other words three inches wide, 6 inches long, and two inches deep. It can be bigger than this but it must on no account be smaller.

It must not be made of cardboard or paper or papier maché

or aluminium or asbestos. It need not be streamlined. It need not have a lock and key. It need not be studded with gems. If it is, the only gem used should be an Alexandrite. I leave the choice of material to you and to your well known taste.

Its fourth dimension is undefined but can perhaps be best indicated by the formula :

$$V \sqrt{\frac{x+y\ (a+b)}{\pi}}$$

I want this as soon as possible. It must not be brittle; on the other hand though it may bend it should not break.

Now as to its moral and temperamental qualities.

@. Racial. It may be Aryan or Mongol, or Eurasian.

b. Nationality. It may be English, Russian, French, Italian, Spanish, Chinese or Basque. But not Scottish Finnish Japanese German Swiss or Belgian. And not Egyptian.

C. Temperament. It must be supple, quick, active, strong, and intelligent : quick at the up take and not *touchy*.

XX D. Epoch. It can be renaissance, antique, not Moyen Age, nor Late Victorian.

It shoud be " sanguin " rather than " Lymphatique."

Now you know.

Miscellaneous Topics.

Is Mr Barton the same man as the man I call Mr Bartlett and then wonder if I have done wrong?

Please tell me. He has some beautiful things in his shop sometimes.

The cold continues to be bitter.

Have you ever read the " Fables de La Fontaine "? They repay the trouble but it is a sign of age to appreciate them.

They are quite unlike the writings of Alfred Lord Northcliffe being more descriptive.

I read one Fable every night and if the Ministers of the Crown did the same they would be wiser men.

I went to High Mass this morning but was called away in the middle like Hernani by the sound of the Claxton Horn of the general's motor car.

Which I at once recognised.

Dieu que le son d'un Claxton est triste sur Un Panhard 120.

The sun shines fitfully, peevishly, grudgingly, stingily untidily.

The rubber rings on the induction pipe cylinder head in the new Raf engine are too hard.
Your loving
    Aviatik.

Head Quarters,
    Royal Flying Corps,   19.6.19.
        B E F France.
Hija de la Belleza!
    Letter received this morning was written in pencil and short.
    I prefer longer letters typed like the one you wrote to Philip which was very neatly typed indeed.
    I wrote you such a long letter yesterday that I never reached the real subject.
    It was this.
    If a flannel shirt, made of good flannel, and not shrinkable *an sich* which has not shrunk after being *properly* washed *several times*, when, is then washed *badly* and returns from the wash *all lumpy with tiny sleeves* is there any further remedy? if washed by a proper blanchisseuse will it recover? Or is the shirt forever ruined and lost beyond redemption?
    Please consult some competent authority and let me know by return of post.
    It is most important.
    I should also like to know what made the shirt shrink.
    It did not shrink for a month when it was properly washed. It is beautiful shirt specially made by Messrs Hummel of Old Bond Street.
    As it is it can never be worn again.
    I wish to prevent this happening to all my shirts.
    The fires are lit and so is the electric light although it is 11 30 A M that is to say really 10 30 A M of the morning of June 19.
    In peace time I suppose this would be the first day of Ascot. And you would be putting on a sober creation in black and yellow and a divine dust coat and a hat so constructed as to excite envy in the hearts of other Bints.
                        Your So-called Morane-Saulnier.

Head Quarters,
            Royal Flying Corps,   20.6.16.
                B.E.F. France.
Chère Entresol,
            I regret to inform you that I received no letter from
you this morning nor indeed from anyone else.
            Oh that I, Oh that I were as the Kingfisher that flies
with untroubled heart over the foam of the sea, (with its
mate), An idle wish.
            Colonel Barres is coming to luncheon.. He squints. The
French call him Dieu le Père because after a spurt of creative
energy he goes to sleep on the seventh day.
            I am sleepy although it is only ten 25 in the morning.
            I am cold although it is the 20th of June.
            I am hungry although I have had breakfast.
            I am ignorant in spite of an expensive education.
            I am foolish in spite of the sound advice I have received.
            I am shortsighted in spite of my excellent eyeglass.
            I am bald in spite of much hairwash.
            I cant do addition subtraction multiplication or long
division.
            I do not know the Signs of the Zodiac .
            I cannot repeat the counties of Scotland.
            The nose-plate of the Clerget engine is too short.
            Oh that I were an acetylene-welder that stands over the
blast of a blue flame and welds precious metals together, XXXX
or if this be asking too much, would I were a fiery jewel, large
and beautiful, needing not the welders flame, and that a
beautiful Bint might wear me having made pure her heart.
                        Yours faithfully,
                            Salter Simpson and Sons,

Head Quarters,
        Royal Flying Corps,
            France.

                                                    20.6.16.

Chère Plusqueparfaite,
            No. Tell Marconivitch that its no use. I wont be
terrorised.

I know perfectly well the difference between Bron's cigarettes and Nans and when I refer to Bron's I mean Bron's and not Nans. If he cant make me or rather wont make a cartridge the size of the sample I sent I dont want any at all. It is no good treating me as if I were the King of Greece and sending me explanations which would make even Bethmann Hollweg blush it wont do.

This is my last word.

Of course I know he is too stupid and too obstinate to make the cartridge or Gilza himself. But why cant he buy some? They are very cheap. Anyone can fill them with tobacco.

Probably the East End is swarming with them.

But no doubt he is too proud and too pig headed and too stupid to do any such thing.

In the meantime my stock of cigarettes is drawing to a close and what will poor Maurice do then? Poor thing?

I believe it is going to be finer today but it is much too early in the morning to tell. The daylight saving stunt makes it impossible for one to tell the time by looking at the sun which is a great nuisance.

Yours Passé Defini.

Head Quarters,
Royal Flying Corps,
B.E.F. France.

22 June 1916

Chere Envergure Totale,

I have been so busy all day that I have not had one minute to write to you and even now I am snatching forbidden time from the Tree of Duty.

If you have any Dramas acted I think the best would be the Aulis thing, the Hangmans Daughter stunt Henry 8 Rosamund possibly and Velasquez.

Henry 8. has been acted twice and acts quite well.

Julius Caesar has been acted several times but I dont care for it on the stage.

I think the Aulis thing and the Hangmans Daughter would be the best. Others have been acted at Cambridge and at the Little Theatre at Chicago.

(Julius Caesar is boring if very badly acted; only the first part was done).

I think it would be great fun. You can do what you like. It was really hot today for the first time for a month. The birds sang and in the wine-coloured clover the poppies flared and the tethered cows munched, while the Moranes looped and the Vickers fought and the Beerbohms Treed.

I am yours with great regard,

Brindejonc des Moulinais.

H.Q.R.F.C.   24.6.16.

Chere Ermengarde,

You are so used to thinking in millions that you can no longer think in inches which is unfortunate.

I want a box Six inches long or *more NOT LESS*.

I want a box Three and a Half inches wide, possibly wider but not less wide.

I want a box at least two inches in depth, possibly deeper but not less deep.

If you figure this out with a tape measure your natural intelligence will tell you that a box of these dimensions unless collapsible could not go into an ordinary pocket.

Indeed I want it for no such purpose but rather to stand four oblong to the winds and broadbased upon the people's will, permanent, solid, unshaken, steadfast, firm, unbiassed, not swayed by the strife of parties or the intrigues of politicians, not vexed by ambition nor haunted by feverish dreams of glory, but self-satisfied, self-schooled, self-controlled, self-sufficing and self-sufficient, and self-esteemed on a table holding or willing to hold at least 250 cigarettes.

It shall never be put in a pocket.

As to the cigarettes, I am willing to buy a thousand cigarettes at the rate of 200 a week on condition that you can get the box as described above; but unless you can get the box the cigarettes are worse than useless.

The box can be made of pure gold if necessary but not of silver nor of bronze. Should it be carved out of a sapphire it should be a star sapphire.

I am your loving Childeric 111.

Head Quarters,
Royal Flying Corps,
B.E.F. France.

25.6.16.

Dear Mrs. Bouverie-Pusey,
        I have read your inquiry into the supposed Mutability
of Animal Types with the greatest interest., It was very kind
of you to send it me.   Your remarks on the permanence of
Evolution are most suggestive.
        With regard to what you about Tableaux Vivants I am
entirely in accordance with you.   I advise you never to go
to another such entertainment.   They are seldom rewarding
and often profitless as well as tedious.
        The weather has been partly fine today and partly thundery.
It rained during the space of a quarter of an hour then it
cleared up.   Do you like condensed milk?   I cannot say I do.
I am dining tonight with Auguste Bréal at least perhaps I am
It depends on the transport as he lives many miles off.
        Dear Mrs. Bouverie, I hope you will have understood the
directions with regard to the Box which I shall call Pandora
as it contains hope and I hope the cigarettes will arrive soon
as without tobacco I am like a cocktail without ice.   Or ice
without a cocktail (Manhattan).
        I am very sleepy,
                Therefore I will say Good Evening,
                        Your most devoted friend and admirer,
                                Mirza Abu Talet Khan.

Head Quarters,
Royal Flying Corps,
B.E.F. France.

26.6.16.

Dear Mrs. Spiers but not Pond,
        Very many thanks for your charming letter which I
received last night.   I mean this morning.
        The rain falls lightly on the lime trees and the wasps are
fed up to the back-teeth.
        The humming bird has stopped humming and the ladybird
has made use of an unladylike expression.

37

But now the sun, rubbing his sleepy eyes, is peering through the clouds which are at about 200; shine out, dear sun; for the music-concert begins and the hour forbids further delay. Therefore Pan, Lord of Arcady and playmate of the nymphs of Bacchus, smile upon my mirth and rejoice in this, my music. This is called a Prose Poem.

> Your Warworn,
> John Keats.

I didnt have dinner with Bréal after all.

Head Quarters,
    Royal Flying Corps,   28.6.16.
        B.E.F., France.
Chere Aérophile,

I picked the first honeysuckle of the season yesterday. There was no bee anywhere near it. Indeed it would be difficult for a bee to live in such wet weather.

Since writing this a lot of things have happened a lot of water has passed under the Bridges. The post has arrived and with it a letter from you. Brindejonc de Moulinais far from living in the days of Henri-Quartre lived in the days of Edouard 7 and possibly, no certainly, in the days of George 5. He is probably alive now. He was and is or perhaps is still a French Pilot one of the early flying men who first ventured in a flying machine in company with Dorothy Deane.

Hence the song "Dorothy Dean where have you been? She's been with the man in the flying machine."

Write often and at length.

I will write when I can.

> Your& Gaspard Hauser.

Head Quarters,
    Royal Flying Corps,   30.6.16.
        B. E. F. France.
Paysage choisi,

      how right you are in what you say about the only kind

of man *à qui on peut se fier*.   How .true this is about Bints
also.   The only kind of Bint *à qui on peut se fier* is the womanly
unpretentious *stupid* Bint.   (Amelia.)   in a word the *good*
Bint.   But Lord deliver us from the *clever* Bint, the *brilliant*
Bint, the *accomplished* Bint, the *political* Bint, the Bint with
charm, the *beautifully-dressed* Bint, the *Beauté-du-Diable* Bint,
in fact the *wicked* Bint.

To which category Isolde no doubt belongs.

How right Tristram was to prefer Isolde of the white hands.
She is a *good* Bint and a *true* Bint and a Bint *one can trust*
and *respect*.   She is the Bint for me.

God give me *good* Bints, *modest* Bints, *womanly* Bints,
simple Bints, *nice* Bints, *kind* Bints, *real* Bints ; and not the
splendid and flashing Bints who are friends of the Devil and
the source of all earthly ills.

The day before yesterday three small boys were found
stealing lace handerkerchiefs with Ypres lace on them, cigarette-
cases, tobacco and cigarettes from the Officers and mechanics
tents.   They were arrested by the sentry and marched into a
tent where they yowled for hours each saying and proving cir-
cumstantially that the other had done it.

Finally Gendarmes arrived.   And they were condemned to
spend the night in the tent and to be whipped the next morning.

I expect they enjoyed it very much.

I am Dear and good Bint,

Your affectionate,
Edwin Clayhanger.

P.S.--Do get Maurice mended.

Head Quarters,
   Royal Flying Corps,   1.7.16.
     B.E.F. France.
Charmante Gabrielle,

I heard from Hillary on his way to the Italian front.   I
think he will enjoy himself.

I have published, did I tell you? a small and boring Gepäck
called *English Landscape*.   I meant it to be sold for the Russian
Prisoners but the publishers said they would rather die than
have a penny of their profits go towards any charity, so I was

reduced to saying that the "compilers profits" if any, would go to the British Fund for the Russian Prisoners of War"; but as you may well imagine, there wont be any compiler's profits. The Publishers will take good care of that. I am supposed to get a penny on every copy sold, so if 5000 copies were sold I should get 5000 pence ie 10000 halfpence or 20000 farthings that is to say 425 shillings or £20 6 shillings and eightpence; but is very unlikely that even 50 copies will be sold in which case I should get 50 pence or 4 and twopence.

Yrs C. N. and A. M. Williamson.

Head Quarters,
Royal Flying Corps,   2.7.16.
 B.E.F. France.
Chere Coccinelle,

Let me know what Hillary says when he comes back from Italy. Make him knurd and elicit from him what he really did. I hope he didnt bother the Italians too much with his religion. That is the last thing they want to be bothered about even the most religious of them. They take it as a matter of course. I am like an old cabhorse. I am like a hoarse and discarded Prima Donna. I am like an out of date fashion plate. I am like a forgotten tune on a cracked barrel organ. I am like a last years Valse. I am like yesterdays toothpick.

Where are the toothpicks of yesterday?

The G. on the other hand is like a young tiger that has just tasted blood and wants to taste more.

Yrs &

Clovis.

Head Quarters,
Royal Flying Corps,   July 2 1916.
British Expeditionary Force,
France.
Princesse Lointaine,

would that the space between us were narrow or nil instead of being immense and inane.

I dont like war.

But then I dont like peace.

In fact I think I like peace less than war.

That is to say when we are at peace I think I am more dissatisfied than when we are at war.

I have been to war three times which for a peaceable civilian is enough. I know what Munthe left out in his description. You can tell him I saw the same things and I too would have been obliged to leave them out. I could indicate them.

No, I shant write a book about what I saw. I havent seen much but what I have seen is never going to be written about

What I have enjoyed most in this war is not having to write about it : the feeling that I hadnt got to write anything except letters to my dear coccinelle.

If possible send me an amusing book small enough to be put in a large pocket. That is to say smaller than a Bible but larger than a Prayer-book and much smaller than a Hymn Book and much larger than a Thumb Dictionary. The more full of senseless gossip your letters are the more I like them but I like them all of whatever kind, and I appreciate their variety. Which is infinite. I have just thrown out of the window Arnold Bennett's book called Edwin and Angelina or words to that effect. I have read bits of it. Do you know Edwin Bennett? You would like him I think.

I didnt throw it out of the window in disgust but as a weapon to hit Major Lawrence who has just come out as a Squadron Commander. He was very pleased and will take away the book and read it. It was the very book he wanted. And this proves the inscrutable ways of Providence.

You wont get such a long letter from me for a long time.

> I went into a provincial town today
> To buy a box of matches.

The air was sweet with the smell of new-mown hay,

I went into a provincial town today.

And on the road I thought of how XXXX Edna May (or Dolly Grey)

> Wore on her chin two patches.

I went into a provincial town today,

> To buy a box of matches.

This is quite true but on the way back the G. said "Give me a match" and I gave. And I never saw the box again. To be without cigarettes is bad; but to be with cigarettes and without matches is worse. The cigarettes I did buy are filthy.

> I saw the new moon rise tonight,
> between the darkling trees,
> Yes half in joy and half in fright,
> I saw the new moon rise tonight,
> O precious fear O dark delight,
> I sniff your aromatic breeze,
> I saw the new moon rise tonight
> Between the darkling trees.

And I remain and beg you to agree the expression of my most devoted hommages,

Geoffroy de Rudel
or Le Prince Lointain.

Head Quarters,
   Royal Flying Corps,   2.7.16.
      B.E.F. France.   [? 2.8.16]
Chère Asti Spumante,

Three or four nights ago a Highland regiment was billeted in our village. Its Colonel lodged in my billet. Their Mess was in the dining room or parlour which was next to my bed-room.

They had to leave for the front before dawn. About two in the morning I was awakened by the noise of boxes being nailed and valises being strapped and by various hammerings, knocks, and by general bustle.

Presently I heard sounds of conversation. The Officers of the regiment's H Q were having some cacao before starting. They didnt talk much. The voices stopped. I thought they had all gone but I all at once heard the voice of the Lady of the house, a grey haired Menagère, who had got up to say Goodbye to them.

She was talking to the Colonel. He was an oldish and mild greyhaired man. I had just caught sight of him the day before.

He spoke French with great difficulty not with a very bad accent but he evidently didnt know many words.   He was thanking her.   He said : "Beaucoup amusé ici."   And she told him that she had been delighted and that his men had behaved so well, especially the cook.   He understood that and said, "Oui 17 ans soldat."   Then she said something simple I think about the weather which he didnt understand and he repeated the word several times and the conversation got into a tangle.   She asked him if he was married and he said " Pas famille," and something else which I didnt hear.   Then he added : "Terrible guerre."   And she said "oui c'est une terrible guerre."   And he repeated "Terrible Guerre."

Then I heard nothing more and fell asleep but I awoke again almost immediately because the regiment was passing the house, the whole Brigade . . . there wasnt a glimmer of light . . . and XXXX horses, guns, carts, ambulances, men . . . men and men . . . went by for hours on their way to the Somme, to go into the line.

Yours intermittently,

Herne the Hunter.

3.7.16.

Dear Mrs. Wareham-Smith,

I have not heard from you since your return your presumed return to London.   Perhaps you have already gone to Wales.

I have read *Sous Verdun* which I liked very much and I am reading *Ma Pièce* which I m not sure I dont like still better.

It is very early in the morning.   Too early to write a letter. But I may not have time later. How exciting all books about the beginning of the war are and how odd it is that they all become dull in just the same way as soon as La Guerre de tranchées begins.   It isnt odd at all but inevitable.

The R.F.C. have been doing extraordinary things; they bomb the Huns day and night.   Every Hun aerodrome is drenched with bombs.   The G. has been marvellous and and wonderfully prescient, if you what that means; if not, look it out in the dictionary.

Yours in hope (of a letter) Woodruff.

3.7.16.

H.Q. R.F.C. B.E.F. France.

Chere Eloise not nouvelle or Willoughby,

I spent the whole day with 2 Squadrons day before yesterday. So as to write reports for the G. directly they came back. It was horrible to have a XXXXXX an amusing luncheon and then to see them go and then to wait and wait and wait. And then they come back sometimes riddled with bullets and sometimes they dont come back. The Squadron Commander I had luncheon with the day before yesterday and saw all yesterday started again this morning and has not come back yet. XXXXXX Sir William Robertson came to luncheon this morning. Do you know him? If not you should. His son is very nice. Mind you nobble Hillary the moment he comes back. I wonder in what sort of clothes or rather in whose clothes he will go and see the Pope. One should go in evening clothes. Perhaps he will borrow a waiter's "clothes." A waiter has no evening clothes. Or rather his evening clothes are our day clothes.

Your most affectionate,

Harold not Hardranger nor Baker and still less Russell.

4.7.16.

Pargoletta,

Of course the push makes a difference to us. It makes the whole difference. We live in a different place, a different house, and do different things and keep different hours. I dread the arrival of the newspapers during a push, with their inane headlines of people being swept out of this, and hurled out of that, and the entirely false perspective they give to everything good and bad.

Their gross exaggerations their silly comments their unreasonable alarms, their hysterical screams of praise or blame.

If I dont get some cigarettes soon I shall give up writing letters altogether. This afternoon there was a heavy thunderstorm. Who is Boris? Not Goudonoff I suppose nor Romanoff. Yes I get your letters quite regularly. They are a bright spot. I am not in a very good temper just now so I cant write you a pleasant letter.

Your last letter received today was very short. My last letter was to you was very long.

If you write me short letters I shall retaliate with asphyxiating gas and chloride of lime.

The latter is the more disagreeable and is plentifully used in this house and garden as a disinfectant.

This is not necessary as there is no epidemic about. There is not even any endemic disease.

Your loving
Crinquebille.

Advance Head Quarters,
    Royal Flying Corps,   5.7.16.
        B.E.F. France.

Chere Eclisse,

I think I shall just have time to write to you before I go out for the day. I have been out once already. Now the wireless has come so this letter must stop till I have dealt with it. I have dealt with it. So I proceed. I enjoyed your last letters which came in a bunch. Bints should be :

GOOD
    KIND.
        DOMESTIC
            EXPERTS IN COOKING
            (NOT IN WINE)
                (IF POSSIBLE BEAUTIFUL)
                    INCAPABLE OF NAGGING
                    Able to sew.
                        ALWAYS READY TO LISTEN
                        Discreet
                            DEVOTED
                                INFINITELY SYMPATHETIC
                    Always ready to go to the Zoo if necessary

I am reduced to smoking asphyxiating gas which is against the Hague Convention.

Goodbye, XXX be good, sweet child, let those who can, be clever,

your loving,
Ralph Rackstraw.

45

Head Quarters
    Royal Flying Corps,
        B.E.F. France.
Objet dont la beauté me ravit a moi-même,
        and I bet you a shilling but not a cent more, that **Eddy**
Marsh, if he doesnt already know, doesnt guess in two guesses
who wrote that line.
    The Flying Corps has been doing magnificent work. One
pilot went out in a single-seater De Havilland and met, rather
he went to meet, as they had been reported, twelve L V Gs.
He went for them and made two turn upside down and fall
headlong, out of control.
    Then he himself was wounded in the thigh. He half lost
consciousness but regaining control over himself, he went for
the others and compelled four of them to land forcibly and
dispersed the rest.
    This fight was witnessed by people on the ground.
    Every day these kind of things happen.
    Write to me definite and accurate news of Bron directly
you know any.
    I have not yet received any cigarettes.
    I have no book to read.
    I have no pen to write with.
    I have no brush to paint with
    I have no peppermint drops to eat.
    I have no raspberry-ade to drink.
    I have no harp to play on.
    I have no Juliet to look at.
    I am solitary unfriended and slow,
                                    Yours nearly,
                                        Montchrestien.

Head Quarters,
    Royal Flying Corps,   8.7.16.
        B.E.F. France.
Chere Juliette Adam,
        I was not satisfied by the letter which I received last
night. It was short and not typed up to standard.
    On the other hand I received two amusing books. One of

46

which was perhaps from you? and from Countess Benckendorff half a million cigarettes. And this last fact has changed the face of the world and made it roseate.

I sang the Te Deum on its arrival I dont care now how long Marconi takes to make the holders.

The weather is absolutely Hellish.

That is all the news there is.

I am with thanks and regards,
                              Your &
                              Quesnay de Beaurepaire.

Head Quarters,
    Royal Flying Corps,   11.7.16.
        B.E.F. France.
Princesse en qui le Ciel mit un esprit si doux,

I much regret to inform you that I received no letter from you today. Possibly as a reward I shall receive two letters or three letters from you tomorrow.

I wish to put on record once more my thanks for the books you sent. They not only give pleasure to me but to others. When I have finished them No 21 Squadron read them and then the mechanics and finally the Anzacs and superfinally the French Interpreters.

I spoke to an Anzac today. They are refreshingly unobsequious.

I hate obsequiosity.

I hate servility.

On the other hand I like to be treated as an equal and not as an Inferior.

In other words I dont like when when I say How do you do to be answered at once by Go to Hell or words to that effect.

The Boshes put up a Notice Board the other day with written on it : "Tell your bloody Flying Corps to leave us in peace, we are Saxons." They werent Saxons. They were Bavarians.

                    Aurevoir,
                        Belle entre toutes les Belles,
                            Votre Bien-aimé,
                                Edwin Capulet.

47

15.7.16.
Head Quarters,
        Royal Flying Corps,
                B.E.F.France.
Chère Liane de Pougy,
    I should be glad of another book. I have read all the books
sent me by kind friends so far. Great Snakes is very funny
I thought. I have never read *At the Back of Beyond.* Is it
good? Have you ever read "Who's Who". It is as Hillary
says admirrrable. Here is an extract from the article on
Janotha.
    "Order of Sun and Lion from Shah of Persia decorated
by the German Empress Vice President of Anti-Vivisection
Society; deported by order August 1915. *Recreations.*
Visiting the chapel of Our Blessed Lady at Czestochowa;
playing the organ, reading great works, mountaineering,
taking care of Prince White Heather (the celebrated cat)."
    Mind you write an tell me what Hillary says on his return.
I should like a full account of his interview with the Pope.
The whole diagnosed by you as to how much of it is true and
how much untrue.
                            Yours truly,
                        Justerini and Brooks.

    17.7.16.
Cher Girofle,
    You must take Maurice to the shop to be oiled if oiled
in the wrong places his tension cord will break that is what
happened to Juliet.
    The French cook has gone. This is what happened. The G
said there was a smell of cooking which there was. Hammond
Gordons servant repeated this to the cook. The cook hit
Hammond in the nose and made it bleed. Gordon spoke
severely to the cook. The cook was rude. The cook was sent
away. So now we have got an English cook who is pretentious
and bad the tepid lawn tennis ball kind.
    You asked for a Sonnet so I instantly wrote one. But it
isnt a good one. One cant always write good ones. It is only
an accident if they are good.

48

Sea-Dream.

I dreamt that you were far away with me,
In shadow sheltered from a blinding light,
And far beneath we watched the seagulls flight,
Through vines that hung above a violet sea.
You plucked me fruit from the pomegranate tree,
I gave you flowers of jessamine soft and white;
The garden was subdued to our delight;
The vine leaves and the ringdove and the bee.
I looked and looked into your endless eyes,
And they were the same colour as the skies,
I was afraid youd break the spell that bound
That Paradise with any mortal word;
But only the lapping waves made a slumberous sound,
And the drone of a bee and the call of a lonely bird.

Brighton. 1916.

Yrs Rominogrobis.

Head Quarters,
    Royal Flying Corps,   18.7.16.
      B E F France.
Cher Entremêt,
      never doubt but that your letters give delight. Every
comma in them is appreciated. Every joke is smiled at.
Every coarse allusion is appreciated. The pathetic parts are
received with tears. The patriotic parts are applauded. Never
were letters so highly prized.

Yours truly,
Hachette et Cie.

Head Quarters,
Royal Flying Corps,   21.7.16.
B.E.F. France.
Cigarette enchantée,
      I am writing as you told me to Paris. Yesterday after-
noon a beautiful box arrived. It is now on my table full to
the brim of slender cigarettes. It is just such a box as I wished

for. It is the box of my dreams. I have christened it Pandora. Juliet, as you see, has recovered. Also I got some writing paper but not very much. Eclectic means fastidious : a person who choses carefully and eliminates all but the very best. A person who likes all sorts of things and who appreciates widely-different things such as for instance Tête de veau Vinaigrette, Bronx-cocktails, sermons in stones, spellicans, dogfights, Shelley, Voltaire, bull-baiting, chess, George Robey, Ibsen, Debussy, Sullivan, Little-Tich, Lebargy, St. Thomas Aquinas, a merrygoround American dentistry and Swedish exercises not forgetting Sauerkraut and Pontet-Canet is a *catholic* person. Harry Cust is the more eclectic but the P M is the more catholic.

Dont say as so many people would " But I thought he was a " Protestant."

Please write me the Paris news in deep detail. Who is staying at the Ritz? Who is not staying at the Ritz? There is no one at the Embassy I much care about.

Yours very truly,
Thomas Cartwright Cullwick.

Recreations : cricket chess.

Address : Norfolk Island via sydney.

Publications : has assisted in translating the Bible into Mota.

H.Q.   R.F.C.   B.E.F.   France.
22.7.16.

Chere Onoto,

Philip and Lord Northcliffe came to luncheon here today. I thought Lord Northcliffe was very like his ancestors. In fact he was like one of the old family portraits come down from the frame. He was most affable. I think he and Hillary would be the greatest friends ; in fact they are very much alike both as to hair clothes and boots. But Lord Northcliffe's manner to strangers is simpler and less elaborate.

Hoping that this finds you as it leaves me
I am yours, in the pink,
Frank Harris.

Recreations. " A lover of books and men who takes pleasure in the past by travelling and in the future by dreaming."

Quoted from " Who's Who "

Head Quarters,
Royal Flying Corps,   22.7.16.
B.E.F. France.
Chère arc-en-ciel nué de cent sortes de soies,
    Alfred Harmsworth, Baron Northcliffe, is here. He is to
visit us tomorrow. Tonight the G. dines with the C in C to
meet him. Hillary should be there also. I always feel that
some day H and Alfred H. will be bosom friends and that H
will say that H is a good man? Do you think that will happen?
Nothing is too extraordinary to happen. The weather is fine
but cloudy.
    Write me all the Paris news and gossip.
    Letter which was going to be long has suddenly been inter-
rupted by pressing business.
                        Yrs sincerely,
                    Kuli Khan (Nawab) Abbas.
                Recreations Stargazing.

Head Quarters,
Royal Flying Corps,   24.7.16.
B.E.F.France.
Chere Oeuf de Paquerette,
        I have got about three minutes to write you in. Firstly
send letters to Avenue Montaigne by Chasseur as if you send
them by post you gain no time but rather lose it. I have been
all day on the battlefield through the German trenches which
we took the other day. It is like a moonscape sprinkled with
poppies and dead Germans' great coats and here and there a
gas mask. Shells were bursting in the distance and our guns
were firing and there was a scream of whistling metal in the
air everywhere. Troops swarming; aeroplanes flying about.
The sky quite grey so that one wondered if one were awake
or not. I think on the whole not. The village of Fricourt
is entirely destroyed that of Mametz is annihilated and there
is nothing left of it but crumbling stones.
        That is all I can tell you at present,
                Cher ami de mon coeur,
                    I remain yours entirely,
            Arthur not Roberts nor Ponsonby nor Balfour but Rex.

Head Quarters,
Royal Flying Corps,   25.7.16.
B E F France.
Cher Oiseau Bleu,
    The sight of the battlefield is amazing. It is one of destruc-
tion on a larger and more systematic scale than has ever occurred
before.
    It is difficult to see in the villages, where the houses were
the ground looks as though it had streams of lava pouring over
it for days out of a red hot volcano. It is pitted with count-
less craters some of them are bright yellow with picric acid. And
the noise goes on without stopping. In the further distance
you see great columns of shell smoke stationary in the air like
permanent geysers only black. In the foreground you see our
guns flashing and when you see the German shells bursting in
the nearer distance you wonder what they are firing at and why.
    Was ever a battle like this fought in the world before?   The
answer is in the negative.
    Perhaps you would like to hear about the new cook. His
food is highly epicé. He puts nutmeg into an omelette and
caraway seed into the soup.
    And he makes patterns round the dishes with bits of salad
and other odds and ends.
    However he gets better every day owing to my indirect but
restraining influence.
    He is told morning noon and night to try and be simple
                    I am your devotedly,
                            Crispin Crispian.

                Head Quarters, Royal Flying Corps,
26.7.16.   B.E.F. France.
Chere Bluette,
        Thank you for two very nice letters which arrived safely
and rapidly yesterday forwarded by Innes-Ker. How long are
you going to stay in Paris? That is what is chiefly pre-
occupying me. I have nothing whatsoever to tell you. The
weather continues to be grey and rather more gloomy than it
was yesterday. I heard from Hillary who has been violently

attacked by H G Wells in the Daily News. H G Wells cannot forgive Hillary for not having been educated at a Board School.

I am yours in all sincerity,
Frank Mildmay.

H.Q. R.F.C. B.E.F. France.
30.7.16.
Voix Celeste,

I received this morning a long and intensely interesting letter from you. I also received from London a writing pad so that I shall be able to continue my correspondence.

Before I say anything else I must put on record that I also like the works of Abel Hermant immensely.

I am looking forward to hearing about your interview with Briand. You did well to buy a new hat for the occasion. But dessous are what he looks at.

No I am not allowed to use the telephone for private conversation. Philip may but not I. Latter must now stop. I may write again later.

Yours very sincerely,
Paul not Saint nor Esterhazy nor Herbert.

I have now got a moment to go on with my letter but I may be interrupted at any minute. Do you think that Barrie would have been happy had he married Madame du Barry? The lilac field of poppies which hitherto flaunted its soft beauty by the side of the road has now faded that is to say the petals have fallen off the poppies. Leaving green nobs.

31.7.16.
H.Q. R.F.C. B.E.F. France.

Aimable fille d'une mère à qui seule aujourd'hui mille coeurs font la cour,

I think by this time you will be back in your comfortable London home not far from your still more comfortable home for soldiers. Let us forget that we must ever part let us also forget we loved each other much.

53

For men must work and women must weep though the harbour bar be moaning. When the Zeppelin was captured in the Thames a dead German who was found inside it was given a naval burial in the rather shallow waters and the parson was told (if he could) to say a few words of German. A few days after this burial the Petty Officer who had carried out these instructions came to the Officer in charge and reported as follows : "Please, Sir, the Un's aflood." I am very sleepy. From 2 to 6 I listened to the troops marching through the village. I am so sleepy that I dont quite know what I am writing. So sleepy that I think I will write no more,

Your loving,

Macbeth, (Beware of Macduff)

6.8.16.

H.Q. R.F.C.

Dear Madame Snelgrove,

I was enchanted to hear from you. The Genitive of plural of oshibka is oshibok. Why it is so I cannot tell. XXXX Yesterday evening a great event took place. Bron flew to France in a flying machine. To our Head Quarters. Not to Advanced Head Quarters. But they telephoned to me and fortunately I obtained permission to go and have dinner there. You can imagine what fun it was. In my excitement I went away without translating the German Wireless. It is fine and clear but cold and the wind is in the North East.

I saw an Australian yesterday who had killed a lot of Germans himself. He said the prisoners as soon as taken devour the hardest biscuits by the hundred such is their voracious hunger.

Thine for ever,

Louis Raemaeker.

7.8.16.

H.Q.R.F.C. France.

Mon cher taxi,

did I get a letter from you yesterday? Alas No. But

54

I did get a letter from the Committee for Prevention of Conscription to Jews which I at once XXX sent to Hillary as being the person most keenly interested in the subject.

I saw the Daily News last Saturday had a huge poster with Naval Airmen Bomb German aerodrome on it. The R F C have bombed a German aerodrome every night and almost every day for the last three weeks including Zep sheds at Brussels and Namur. Besides stations and junctions. Juliet as you see had a fainting fit but I called in an expert who gave her a hypodermic injection and now she is all right again.

Your in adoration Gorner Grat.

H.Q. R.F.C. B.E.F. France.
  10.8.16.
Belle Amie,

Yesterday I received no letter from you nor from any one else save a Note from the War Office and a Circular asking for a subscription to the Ellen Terry fund for Homesick Cannibals. Imagine my disgust more than disgust, the almost intolerable wave of surging bitter despair. I felt just as Tristan did when Iseult told him she had really been in love with King Mark the whole time. I felt like Columbus when after his long and dreary voyage he was told it wasnt America, the place where he had landed, but the Isle of Man. In the meantime I have lost your Welsh direction will you send it to me? Vaynol or Odol or Veronal which was it? It is raining gently but firmly. Last night the whole sky was covered with soft billows of clouds like a ploughed field or a sea of pearl.

I remain Yours in disgust
Hans Pless. (Not Place.)

Head Quarters,
  Royal Flying Corps, B.E.F. France.
    11.8.16.
Dolce Sirena,

I have only a moment to write to you this morning.

This letter may stop at any minute. It is living on a volcano. It is fiddling while Rome is burning.

All sorts of stunts are going to happen today about which I will tell you later or perhaps not at all. I have come to an end of all my books. I am reduced to reading an old Cheque Book.

The fields now are yellow with standing corn. Some of it has been cut. And the grasshopper of Lacedaemon is ready for the dance.

I remain,

Yours patiently,

Brougham and Vaux.

Head Quarters, Royal Flying Corps, B.E.F.
France.
13.8.16.
Torch-bearing Daughter of Night the dark Bosomed,

I have a great piece of mews for you not horse mews but a piece of news. I have let my rooms in Grays Inn. The contract is signed. It is a great weight off my mind just as it was a weight off your mind when you found you were not obliged to buy a house that was situated in the middle of a bankholiday with a cesspool underneath it. Let us both be thankful that the follies we commit are ultimately remedied and erased by a kind Providence. I hope to hear from you today. David Henderson is here. I am going out with him this afternoon. It is not a very fine day. Nevertheless the aeroplane (B.E. 12. Monoplane 12 cylinder Raf) is winging its way in the harvestless inane.

Yours surely, De Horsey.

(Admiral.)

Head Quarters,
    Royal Flying Corps,   15.8.16.
        B.E.F.France.
O vous! Iris, qui savez tout charmer,

David has just gone. I think his visit has done him good.

The other day at luncheon with D Henderson M Poincare and Joffre were there and Joffre was offered the choice between Lemonade and Ginger Beer. He was at first dumbfounded and then said plaintively to the waiter which ever you like. He entirely depends on his luncheon. He feels like Hillary about wine. I think it is very silly to carry your whims into foreign countries and to force them on to foreign people dont you think?

Yours wholeheartedly
Coquelin (FilsX)

Head Quarters,
    Royal Flying Corps,   17.8.16 P.M.
      B.E.F.France.

Patera gemmis corusca,

you complain of prosaic forms of address in my letters to you. But surely you know that letters, the only letters worth getting, are those which are the creatures of impulse and the offspring of moods. This being so, it follows that the forms of address with which they begin and with which they will end, must necessarily vary according to the mood of the writer. My letters to you are written nearly always in the early morning between 8.45. and 9. At nine they have to come to an abrupt end.

At that particular time of the day I am below normal physically, below XXXX all depths of depression morally, and non-existent intellectually. Sometimes, very rarely, as now, I can write to you in the evening. But then I suffer from extreme fatigue.

This is all to say that the forms of address must be, and must remain, as they are, and as they come. Sometimes they will be poetical as today's (which you will not understand) and sometimes they will be prosaic and sometimes you may even be addressed as Mrs Askwith or worse still as Mrs Asquith twice running. It might even happen that you might be invoked as Mr Asquith or as Mr Askwith.

Yesterday a man was staying here who comes from the War Office and works in the same department as Evan. Evan told him that I wrote him very long and very dull letters.

57

The other man said "surely as he writes such good books he must write good letters" (Never did any thing follow less) upon which Evan said : "NO, he writes the dullest of letters." Although this is quite true I think it releases me from any obligation to write to Evan, dont you? The tiresome part is that Evan writes me, when he does write, VERY AMUSING letters ; so that if I stop writing to him I shall not get his letters anymore, and as I only write letters to get letters, I should be cutting off my bootlaces to spite my boots.

I am more tired than words can express. I wish I were in Wales, at Vaynol near Bangor on the road to Helllwelllllllyn. But I am not. Yours regretfully,

Henri Standish.

H.Q. R .F.C.
B.E.F.France.
19.8.16. 8.30.A.M.
Del mattino la fresca rosa,

I am sorry your gardener suffers from epilepsy but if one remembers that Caesar, Napoleon, Dostoyevsky and Spinoza all suffered from the same ailment there is no need to grumble.

It was a year yesterday that T. took over command of the R F C. What he did with such difficulty and in face of such opposition is now admitted by all to have been triumphantly successful, and during these operations his genius has been proved.

And every one admits it. The French think he is a wonder. They say "C'est quelqu'un" which is the greatest praise dont you think?

I remain yours disobediently,
Jean 2 dit le Bon.

Head Quarters,
Royal Flying Corps,   19.8.16
B E F France.
Adorable Place Pigalle,

I only saw the K in the extreme distance. I just caught

58

a flash of his effulgence and that was all. Yesterday I had a headache all day. This morning I feel slightly better. I recommend you to read Lord Granvilles Correspondence or Lady Bessboroughs I forget what it is called and I havent read it myself yet but I intend to.

Charles Peguy was and is very much admired by the French Literary nuts except by those who wrote prose and verse themselves they couldnt abide him. And let me tell you this is not necessarily an indication of jealousy but means that a great artist cannot tolerate the methods of another great artist. It is only mediocre writers like myself who float ecstatic on an ocean of catholic admiration. The second crop of roses here is fine.

Yours still Waters run deep.

Head Quarters,
Royal Flying Corps, B.E.F. France.
    29.8.16.
Chère et plus que chère,

I received a long and amusing letter from you. Do not hestitate to tell me news. I dont mean how the peace is going on and what the Ministers say nor who has got Ireland nor what Winston is thought to be going to do next but news about yourself and your doings : what you had for tea, where you drove to, where you bathed, if the motor car broke down, who is staying with you, what they said and did, and what you said and didnt. I wish to hear all about that.

I am your expectant friend,
Abethedin.

Head Quarters,
Royal Flying Corps,   31.8.16.
B.E.F. France.
O Sole mio,

The gale is over. The clouds have been blown away. The sky is clear. The sun is shining.

The sky is thick with flying machines.

The battle is proceeding. The partridges are anxiously awaiting the morrow which is the first of September Der Tag. They are thinking of joining the allies.

Your Toc.

Head Quarters,
    Royal Flying Corps,   3.9.16.
        B.E.F. France.
Pelegrina Rondinella,
       You ask me whether I prefer a long letter or a short letter. I prefer a long letter to a short letter. But I prefer a short letter to no letter. No, I am not reading Shakespeare just at present. I am reading the complete works of O. Henry who is the American Shakespeare and the American Chekhov and the American Gorki and the American Kipling. And the American Maupassant. I hope you will become a garden bore. Garden bores are the nicest of bores.

In the meantime it is not very fine. I saw Lord Derby this morning and shook hands with him. Fancy shaking hands with a real Lord.

I dont like the anti-fly spray. It smells of lessive and I think it is worse than flies and I strongly disrecommend you to get one.

You have written to me every now and then about Guillmer but I should like to point out that we have in our flying corps a youth called *Ball* who since the operations (what you call the push) has brought down 21 Boche machines, by brought down I mean he has *seen* them crash. The other day he brought one dowm Boche and flew down to 100 feet to make sure what had happened to it over the Boche lines. The Archies, our Archies, saw him go down and reported him shot down, and he was reported missing to his Brigade but having noted that his enemy was a wreck and a pulp or what is picturesquely called by pilots "a dog's dinner," he, Ball, flew gently home and went to bed. He also brought down two Kite Balloons on the same afternoon a feat thought to be impossible and he went out a third time to shoot a third but missed it. His machine in rags and tatters.

Yrs O. Henry

Head Quarters,
Royal Flying Corps,   4/9/16.
B E F France.

Gazza Ladra,

The weather forecast says Some showers at first. I suppose the some showers are going on as it has poured with rain steadily since one in the morning.

At this moment a motor bicycle exploded in the yard with a loud report entirely breaking the thread of my argument. I forget what I was saying. On such a morning as this Columbus was sorry he discovered America on such a morning as this Napoleon kicked Talleyrand in the stomach on such a morning as this Anthony quarelled with Cleopatra and Giotto had to use a compass.

It is therefore unreasonable of you to expect that I should go on writing.

I am yours profoundly Dismal Jimmy.

Head Quarters,
Royal Flying Corps,   6/9/16.
B.E.F. France.

Seraphim du soir,

today two years ago the British Army began to advance and the Battle of the Marne was already in progress since yesterday at midday, when XXXXX Maunoury attacked on the Ourq. This day two years ago I was on the road not to Mandalay but to Touquin where I suffered the irreparable loss of my notebook. This day a year ago I was at a chateau which had been (a) the Head Quarters of the Duke of Marlborough (b) the Head Quarters of the Duke of Wellington (c) the Head Quarters of the First Cavalry division of Field Marshal Frenchs Army.

So much for retrospection and History and the past. Now for the present.

Today the Prime Minister of England comes to tea with us.

The final of the Squadron Coit-Tennis championship was played last night in No. 27 Squadron. Who won it? Thats a secret.

Tonight I am dining with Colonel Hoare at or rather in a

beautiful chateau where there is a long avenue of immemorial trees full of the moan of immemorial doves and the murmuring of unsophisticated bees. The tapestry on the chateau walls is old and faded like the leaves of pear trees at the end of September. The rooms are vast. The chimney pieces elegant, the woodwork simple but beautiful and dignified. In the house lives a peevish Marquis. He is over 80 and his temper is such that when the Anzacs shot his hens and his ducks with revolvers he came out in his night shirt into the farmyard and quelled them till they quailed before the vehemence of his invective. He is looked after by a Boche nurse. She is a pure-sang Boche and very old too and not even the fact of France being at war with Hunland would cause him to be separated from his nurse. Boche or no Boche, he said she remains here till I die.

But she with crafty intent beareth in the one hand water and in the other fire. Nevertheless he will never be false to the great oath and to the salt and table of hospitality but rather he sits upon a couch in the midst of good cheer, a stone overhanging him, seeing nothing but like to one who thinks he sees, while overhead the aeroplane, broad-winged and mobile wings its way in the harvestless inane. (Νωμᾶται δ' ἐν ἀτρυγέτῳ χάει.)

I think the right policy is to write letters to as many people as possible and then one ends by getting a lot of letters. Yesterday I got four. Two of them were from you the third was a bill from the Corona Company and the fourth was a circular from the Home for Unselfish Caterpillars.

There are slight signs of it clearing up. H G Wells came here yesterday on his way back from the Italian front and after having spent a few moments with the French. He had got a bad cold. He was dog tired with large black pouches under his eyes and the look of a man who has been shown and explained things till he can no more. I took him to see the aeroplane repair section of the Second Aircraft Depot in which he took an intelligent interest as far as he was able to be interested in anything. But I didnt let him see too much and gave him tea which partially revived him. He was in charge of the son of Lady de Trafford whom you may have heard of. I mean Lady de Trafford not the son.

Yours very truly,

Beast-tending Pan.

Head Quarters,
        Royal Flying Corps,   6/9/16.
            B.E.F. France.
Fior della mia pianta percossa ed inaridita,
        Mr. Asquiths visit went very well.   He saw the little
birds at their work and the men going out to fight Boches and
others coming back after having fought Boches.   Among the
latter was Ian Henderson, who came back with his face black
with the smoke of battle.
        I am obliged to stop.   I remain your captive,
                                            Simple Cymon.

Head Quarters,
        Royal Flying Corps,   11.9.16.
            B.E.F. France.
Deh bella Donna,
        the news is that an Army Order is about to be pub-
lished according to which in future the shaving of the Upper
Lip will be optional but the Knut or Toothbrush moustache
will no longer be tolerated.   This seals the doom of Brons
moustache.   I must write and tell him today.   I wonder what
the Germans will think of this and what their countermove
will be.   They may possibly sack Hindenburg.
        I wrote 20 letters yesterday mostly to shops
        Shops are I find the best correspondents although they are
sparing of news.
                                            Yrs A. Men.

14 September 1916.
        H Q R F C B E F France.
Etoile d'amour ne descends pas des cieux,
        but write to me.   It is really a fine morning and this is
astonishing as the weather prophet said it was going to be misty.
        Your country house and surroundings sound beautiful.
Especially the seagulls and the the sunsets.   You live between
the sunset and the sea.   I had a very nice dinner last night with
No. 27 Squadron.   There is an Australian in their Squadron

called Steve he is very nice and feeds entirely upon cayenne pepper. I like all Australians. I " find " them Nice.

I am beginning to think that one of the greatest advantages an Englishman can have is not to have been to a public school. Of course it is best for the majority to go to public schools but when you come across some one who hasnt been to one they are generally refreshingly exceptional.

The summer does not mean to have any truck with us as long as the war lasts.

Even the wasps have gone to a neutral country. And what is summer without wasps?

You may wonder why I take such interest in the weather. I think of nothing else. Only people in the Flying Corps know what the weather is really like and whether it is fine or not.

And now my golden hearted shining faced Bint,
> I must stop,
>> and subscribe myself
>> your loving Wingle wangle.

16/9/16.
Head Quarters Royal Flying Corps,
    B.E.F. France.
Estrella de mi noche,

I have got neither box nor drawer I can lock. The result is that I can keep no letters at least not the kind of letters I get. They are too " cynical " to be left about. It is true I have an attache case what is called an Attache case and it had a key but I lost it and the shop couldnt send a new one or wouldnt.

Net result I have to burn my letters unless they are business letters. I think you are right about cynicalness. But the man who said the Block was cynical said it not because the Block had made a joke but because he had said something quite serious about the war. I know Raymond isnt at all cynical. Harry Cust isnt. I think Linky is. All the Cecils have got something cynical in their nature inherited from Queen Elizabeth.

But really as to the Block I have no idea Is he cynical or is he not? That is the question.

Yesterday was a terrific day. The airnarod brought down

24 Boches and did 2000 hours flying in the day.   Ball brought down what is his 23rd or 24th machine.

Trains were exploded in half.   Infantry and batteries fired on, as well as stations roads aerodromes junctions chateaus trains in motion and rolling stock.

One train was made to go off like a box of fireworks.   All the soldiers got out and then they dropped an enormous bomb right in the middle of them.

Terrible Guerre, child of mine.

Arent Julian and Billys letters wonderfully beautiful?

I think that book is unique.   Do you remember the night you and I and Billy went to lady Ottoline Murrels?

Let me know when Michael goes to school and where.   By the way I got no letter from you yesterday.   A great disappointment.   Lady Bessborough says in her letters that the greatest disappointment in the world is to expect a full post and to get none.   Great things are happening at this very moment.   I have come to end of my books being a fast reader by nature.

Hasta la vista,
        Macgillycuddys Reeks.

17 9 16.
H.Q. R.F.C. B.E.F. France.
Chère chère,
        I have just heard that Raymond has been killed.   I felt quite certain the last time I saw him that he would be killed   I am bitterly no just not bitterly but profoundly sorry but I dont think it a waste.   I think it is no more a waste than for someone to give the best kind of gift they have got to someone they are engaged to be married to.

I recommend "Heart of the West" by O. Henry.

I am sorry Raymond has been killed.   I am sorry Raymond has been killed.   I can think of nothing else.

I am glad the Block saw him the other day.   I didnt see the picture in the Daily Sketch.

Send it me.   Will you?

I am sorry Raymond has been killed.

Yours . . . "I find I am finished"
        P. Charles.

18/9/16.
H.Q. R.F.C. B.E.F. France.
Chere Aubepine,
   it is pouring with rain so you wont expect either a long or a cheerful letter.

Indeed it would be difficult to describe the intense gloom of such a Monday morning. But I hope it may clear up. I hope and hope and hope and shall continue to hope against all hope.

The whole atmosphere of life is darkened by Raymonds death.

I must stop.
    Yours Albert the Naughty.

H.Q. R.F.C. B.E.F. France.
  20/9/16.
Étincelle de joie,
   I can still only think of Raymond. Did you know him well?

I have just written to some of them.

What will Katharine do? As for him I think his death the most splendid achievement of his life. He had so much more to give than anyone and he gave it so splendidly.

Osborns brother is in his regiment. I hope he has not been killed.

The G. has just come into the room like a tornado shouting Certainly Not about some memorandum written for him of which he has only read one sentence.
    Yours Toto chez Tata.

20/9/16. H.Q. R.F.C. B.E.F. France.
Chou fleur au gratin,
   Yesterday I made the acquaintance of Guillemer. He is young and exactly like a sparrow. You want to know him. You make a fuss about him. Why dont you make a fuss about Ball who has had 86 fights in the air and brought down 24 Huns for certain. He is also quite young 22 or 20.

I liked Guillemer very much.

As a rule no very good pilot lasts very long even if he is not killed in the air or in the sea or by accident.

And as for that which cometh from Zeus there is no clear sign in Heaven that waiteth on man yet we build high designs yearning after many exploits; for our limbs are fettered by hope and the tides of foreknowledge are hidden from us. And in our heart is a blind desire.

Do you like le style élevé or do you prefer the simple-prattle-of-the-fireside-kettle style?

Do not hesitate to send the latest news about your garden.

Your respectful Alpacka,

Head Quarters,
Royal Flying Corps,   22/9/16.
    B E F France.

Ewig weibliche,

Ball brought down two more Boches yesterday.

This hero is praised by the prudent. I shall only say what is said by others. He cherisheth a mind and a tongue that are beyond his years; in courage he is like a broad-winged eagle among birds, and even from his mothers lap he has soared among the clouds and all the openings around him for noble exploits hath he boldly tried.

He flies a Nieuport single seater with Rhone engine and he cleans his machine himself and dopes it himself with acetone that hath a pungent smell.

He has had now nearly ninety fights in the air. And he still rejoices in the fighting and the flying thinking lightly of it.   Yours always, San Remo.

Head Quarters Royal Flying Corps,
    B.E.F. France.
24/9/16.

Cher Nid D'Abeilles,

you will be sorry to hear that the epicyclic gearing of the the hand starter on the 250 Rolls R E 7 has gone wrong. That is all my news.

Navarre the french pilot has been just let out of prison into which he had been put and kept for insubordination. His rebellion took the shape of his throwing all his medals into his C O s face. The moment he got out of prison he celebrated his release by getting into a machine and doing a spinning nose dive from 200 feet but as was to be foreseen the machine simply went crashing into the ground. He escaped with a bruise. I have come to an end of all my books.

Yesterday a man in a Martinsyde charged a Boche and sent the Boche to the ground like a stone but in so doing his own ailerons were cut away. He got back over our line but couldnt land and had to run into a tree. He dislocated his shoulder. It was a marvellous achievement that he was able to get back. The fight happened over Cambrai. As for me I rejoice in voicing the triumphant praise that befitteth such an exploit. The fame of glorious deeds grows even as when a tree shoots forth beneath refreshing dews; even so is fame borne aloft to the liquid air among men among the good and the just.

A bird is piping in the garden and one pink rose is hanging on the rose tree, and the wasps, an idle brood, are wasting their time and mine.

And from afar comes the echo of the war shout, the daughter of war, the prelude of spears, to whom soldiers are sacrificed for the sake of their city in the holy sacrifice of death.

That being so I remain . . . I have read the Joyeux Garcon. I like it pretty well. I like the Rat still better but also pretty well. Neither tale completely satisfies the fastidious taste and the critical spirit of

Your whole hearted acquaintance and immemorable friend,

C. Roberson. (Lien-faced)

ie Linen-faced

Head Quarters,
Royal Flying Corps,   24/9/16.
B.E.F. France.   No, not at all 25.
Venus toute entière,

many thanks for your letter written in ink yesterday. The story of Michaels school going went to my heart. You dont seem to have cared one scrap. The hard-heartedness of

Bints is amazing. They are like flints. Also I may as well tell you that grown up people have no no no idea what a school is like by looking at it from the outside and boys dont tell them till they are themselves grown up. Parents go and say "What a charming school! how well arranged! how homely! how *happy* the boys look! what a *charming* man Dr. Girdlestone is! while in reality Dr. Girdlestone is a narrowminded violent unbalanced almost lunatic fanatic, a tyrant and a persecutor . . .

In spite of all this at most schools the boys however bad the school is are fairly happy. For one thing they think that *is* happiness. Secondly they have great fun in spite of and perhaps because of the masters.

I suppose now at schools all the masters are dug outs!

Yours Covey Stenning.

H.Q. R.F.C. B.E.F,France.

28/9/16.

Divinite du Styx,

yesterday I got two letters from you which made up in a certain degree for not having had any the day before.

George Moores Gospel according to George and Mary Hunter is a very tiresome book just like any rewritten Gospel and most "historical" novels. It is full of local colour and builded up atmosphere and documents. And the result is that the central figure ends by being exactly like a Holman Hunt picture.

Such is the irony of God which cannot be escaped from even by the literary.

I remain yours ever hopeful but sometimes peevish,

Golden Drop.

Head Quarters, Royal Flying Corps, B E F France.
2/10/16.
Divinest patroness,

it is raining slightly. Bron is supposed to arrive today. I shall probably see him soon.

69

I have almost finished Twelfth Night. Yesterday I saw Ball. I asked him how many Boches he had shot down. He said he didnt know. He didnt count them. He knew he had shot down twenty. He is a dark little man with eyes of fire. I liked him very much. Last night I had dinner with George Lawrence at No 70 Squadron. We talked about a lot of things. He likes O. Henry very much. I dont think you need have travelled to appreciate O. Henry but you need a certain dose of human nature. After dinner we drank Old Brandy till we were senseless. Then I flew home. In the dark. I was not afraid to go home in the dark besides which I had an electric lamp. I forgot to tell you that the shock absorber on the tailskid of the Spad is too *fierce*.

Your serene Highness.

Head Quarters,
    Royal Flying Corps,
        B.E.F.France.
        2/10/16.
Chère Vache d'Or,
    With regard to actors here are my views.
    I find famous actors the most tiresome company the most uninteresting the most colourless in the world. I admit they have admirable qualities such as generosity and kindness but I think they are never amusing and never intelligent in conversation but much the reverse.
    And this is due to (a) the gradual blotting out of their individuality, their way of taking the stage and to something else which it would be wrong to call conceit as it is something far greater but at the same time something less noxious than conceit a quality which has the effect of blotting out for them the whole universe with the exception of their theatrical exploits. This includes b and c.. B being the pose C the quasi-conceit which is more and less than conceit.
    On the other hand minor fairly obscure average hardworking professional actors I have always found simple unselfish and obliging.
    These I like.
    On the other hand God knowing all this well and thinking

that Hillary and others might become too contemptuous of actors took care to make Shakespeare an actor and Moliere an actor. The greatest French writer and the greatest English writer. For I dont suppose you believe that Bacon wrote Shakespeare or that Bossuet wrote the plays of Moliere. But such hypotheses are born of the natural contempt in which the actors profession is held by humanity at large.

Shakespeare himself wrote of the actors profession in turns of burning scorn. See Sonnet CX Alas t is true I have gone here and there and made myself a motley to the view and in Sonnet CXI where he talks of public means that public manners breeds.

Thence comes it that my name receives a brand
And almost thence my nature is subdued
To what it works in like the dyers hand

This is the fate of all actors. Their nature is subdued till they have no nature left at all. The powder and the grease paint chokes their individuality.

Here I quite agree with Hillary. Were you to go on the stage I should be stunned with regret shame and anger and sorrow.

I would rather see my nieces dead than on the stage. XXXX Although I do not think that actors and actresses are worse than other people but sometimes much better I think the process of the dyers hand for them is stronger and to resist it they have to be Shakespeare or Moliere. I think in other words that the stage is a terrible ordeal and I know that all actors and actresses agree with me. They have recorded their opinion to this effect. Ask any of them whether they want their children to go on to the stage and they say No with one voice.

Mrs Kendal may be much more respectable than Lady Strawberry. That is not the point. The point is the brand and are the successes of the stage worth the brand? I think not.

Another point about actors and actressess. Few of them succeed in learning how to act. That is all I have to say on the subject.

Please write and tell me of other conversations that occur at your dining table. Yours in friendship and good will,

Will.

Head Quarters,
Royal Flying Corps,
B.E.F.France.
5/10/16.

Chere Athenée,

in spite of the faultiness of the ribbon which you see
is faint indeed I am compelled to write to you. I dont know
Hillary's poem about Queen Mary and as I havent got his
serious or indeed any book of his here whether serious or comic
I cant look it up. I didnt know he had ever written a poem
about Queen Mary. The soap I told you arrived. It is soft
sensuous and impassioned. The three qualities indispensable
to soap.

I have not yet seen Bron.

I have just read King Lear. I think you are more like
Goneril than Regan and more like Regan than Cordelia. But
you have many qualities that none of these three sisters
possessed such as being able to plant wallflowers.

It is a probable play. It is the kind of thing which might
happen any day and I daresay it happens in the east end
very often. And one feels it was bound to happen.

The people get carried away by themselves

It begins with a family row and all family rows are capable
of leading to such things unless firmly 'checked or unless
there are enough doors to bang. I know exactly what the
Morning Post meant about Leek Taffy and I suppose you do
now. I do not believe your other alarmist tale.

I believe nothing.

But I believe in a good many things including God.

Your nicely, Tamerlane.

Head Quarters,   8/10/16.
Royal Flying Corps,
B.E.F. France.

Chere Impédance,

My mind feels the usual stagnation of Monday
morning. Why is Monday morning under a peculiar curse?
I cannot think. It is dark grey cloudy misty sullen damp and

72

"mild." A horrible spectacle. I with my usual optimism hope it will clear up. My hope is not shared by the weather prophet but then he seldom tells the truth.

I was able to get Bron three Valve rockers old type for the 120 Beardmore engine and to get them for him at once which was satisfactory.

Bron is in a good Squadron and he is as happy as a bird I mean an aviator.

General Allenby arrives in half an hour to be shown a few interesting items.

Mr. Geoffrey Robinson and Sir Philip Sassoon visited us yesterday.

> I remain yours in bondage,
> Kuno Fisher.

Head Quarters,
Royal Flying Corps,   15.10.16.
    B.E.F. France.
Chok gusel Bulbul,

I dont understand. I have written to you about the writing paper the attache case and the salts and you dont appear to have received any of these letters. Perhaps the German submarines are getting busy and are at fault. Perhaps my letters have been confiscated at the Base. Perhaps the Welsh Post has sent them to Lloyd George on approval. Perhaps your parrot has stolen them. All I can do is to go on writing.

Yesterday Bron came to luncheon. He is enjoying himself tremendously. We spent a happy afternoon in the Aircraft Depot looking at various spare parts and repairs and new machines. We also visited the stores.

There were some Dacian prisoners at work. By Dacian I mean Prussian. One of them said he had been Hotels secretary at the Hotel Adler Berlin and also for a year at the Hyde Park Hotel London.

Fancy that.

Give me the sun . . .

> Your thirsty,
> Oswald.

16/10/16.
Head Quarters, Royal Flying Corps, B.E.F. France.
Lilium Aureum,

I am very sorry your Owl is dead. Very sorry indeed. Lugete Veneres. Juliet's owl is dead. Juliet's Owl has flown down to a darker shadow and a Twilight unhaunted by any star. Juliet's owl has gone to meet the birds that were beautiful and are no more. Juliet's owl who was wise beyond his years and in figure and face like an ambassador has gone to hoot in the silver woods that glimmer in'the everlasting darkness. Juliets owl will flit round the eyes of Prosperpine's window and roost in the orchards of Hecate. But nevermore shall Juliet see her owl again and play with him and fondle him, the downy one, the playful, the infinitely precious.

Therefore, Muses and Graces weep for Juliet; but for her owl shed no tears, for he released at last from a woman's fickle whim and irksome caresses is flying unfettered in Elysian woods and feasting where he lists and when he pleases on that food which of all others he prefers.

Nevertheless weep for Juliet who is crying because she no longer has an owl to tease and to torment. Forsooth he was a pretty bird.

Your sympathetic,
Mustang.

Head Quarters,
Royal Flying Corps,   18/10/16.
B.E.F. France.

ELEGY ON THE DEATH OF JULIETS OWL.

Juliet has lost her little downy owl,
The bird she loved more than all other birds.
He was a darling bird, so white, so wise,
Like a monk hooded in a snowy cowl,
    With sunshy scholars eyes;
He hooted softly in diminished thirds,
    And when he asked for mice,
He took refusal with a silent pride
    And never pleaded twice.

74

He was a wondrous bird, as dignified
    As any Diplomat
    That ever sat
By the green table of a Conference.
He was delicious, loveable and soft.
He understood the meaning of the night
And read the riddle of the smiling stars.
    When he took flight
    And roosted high aloft,
Beyond the shrubbery and the garden fence,
He would return and seek his safer bars,
All of his own accord, and he would plead
Forgiveness for the trouble and the search
And for the anxious heart he caused to bleed,
And settle once again upon his perch
And utter a propitiating note
    And win the heart
Of Juliet by his pretty winning ways.
    His was the art
Of pleasing without effort easily.
    His fluffy throat,
    His wise round eye
Sad with old knowledge, bright with young amaze,
  Where are they now, Ah where?
Perchance in the pale halls of Hecate,
Or in the poplars of Elysium,
He wanders careless and completely free.
    But in the regions dumb,
    And in the pallid air,
He will not find a sweet caressing hand
Like Juliet's; nor in all that glimmering land
Shall he behold a silver planet rise
As splendid as the light of Juliet's eyes.
Therefore in weeping with you, Juliet,
    Oh let us not forget
To drop with sprigs of rosemary and rue,
    A not untimely tear
    Upon the bier
Of him who lost so much in losing you.

M.B.

Head Quarters,
Royal Flying Corps, B.E.F. France.
21.10.16.
Chere Limite d'Elasticite,
(Point maxima de deformation elastique a laquelle peut atteindre un corps soumis a la pression de forces exterieures)
I think the cold weather also laudable praisworthy desirable necessary convenient suitable and a Godsend in every way does have a deplorable effect on tempers. The Cure in the village has I think gone mad. He refuses to say Mass at a stated time and never says it twice running at the same time in case someone should go to it. Je ne dis pas la Messe pour la Paroisse. This morning he said Mass at half past six and refused to ring the bells for it. You might consult Hillary about what can be done. Nothing I fear. It is a great bore and very inconvenient. I went to Mass as usual its being Sunday and found no Mass and several people waiting who presently realised the situation and went away. I may add that Mass is announced on the Slab in the Church as being at 8 on Sundays and 7 30 on week days. In point of fact it happens at any odd hour when the Cure feels inclined. Is a Cure allowed to do this? The other people including my landlord were highly indignant. My landlord said Il est un peu original vous savez which I suppose was a polite way for saying that he was raving mad.

A J B is coming to visit us.

That is all I have to say at present.

Your Frozen,
Roderick Dhu.

Head Quarters, Royal Flying Corps,
B.E.F. France.
23.10.16.   This date is correct.
Chere Perle Noire,
Thank you for two short and plaintive letters in which you say you wish you were dead. We all wish that at times. Nevertheless we continue to go on. And every now and then we enjoy ourselves. Forgive me for offering you such tedious consolation. I was genuinely sorry about the owl and I

expressed my sympathy to you in many modes.   But you were merely slighted by my clumsy attempts and I merely made sorer the wound which I hoped to pour balm on.   Such is the vanity of human intention.   Mr. Balfour came here yesterday and was shown things in the air and on the ground.   He was much interested I think and most kind and delightful to everybody.

As for me I had a bath last night in a piece of india-rubber —a kind of cockle shell—and into that unsteady and wobbling receptacle I hurled the rich bath salts tasting of Rothschild and of Jermyn Street.   And very nice it was.   Il naufragio mé dolce in questo mare, as Leopardi the saddest of poets, said.

      Your abiding,

              Keith of Ravelstone.

12 Quotations Unusual.

1. Shadowy isles of bliss mid most the beating of the steely sea.
2. Le pouvoir ne grandit que les grands.
3. Celui qui a crée le monde doit être bien bête ou bien méchant.
4. Come hither in thy hour of strength
   Come hither like a breaking wave,
5. Mrs. Gill is very ill and nothing can improve her
   Unless she sees the Tuileries and waddles round the Louvre.
6. A bare brown stone by a babbling brook,
   It was wanton to hurl it there you say.
7. For Gods sake hold your tongue and let me love.
8. "And faithless lovers in the fires of Hell
   Shall kindle one anothers dead desire."
9. Undeserved rewards are exquisite.
10. Donne moi le remos afin que Je puisse gouter le plaisir.
11. Alle uebel brachten Aepfel.
12. Quel demon sur la terre.

Soufle dans tous les cœurs la fatigue et la guerre.

This is too well known so as alternative

      You the strong sons of anger and the sea

      What weakness on the wings of battle flew?

Head Quarters Royal Flying Corps, B.E.F. France.
  26.10.16.
Dear Mrs. Potter Brown,

I have just got a long letter from you and I am quite sure I prefer a long letter to a short one. I do like Fleckers poems : one or two very much indeed. The Old Ships is I think magically beautiful also the Ballad of Iskander and one called Stillness. or to be more accurate Stillness. Since writing this I have been interrupted by a General. I have also tried to find the Noailles poems. And failed. I wanted to reread the third one which I have entirely forgotten. All I can find is the long one which leaves me cold in a palace of admiration.

Now I can go on. . . We had luncheon today at Lorraine's Squadron. Lorraine the actor. His whole Squadron was "produced" and stagemanaged as though it were the second act of "The Squadron Commander" a comedy in three Acts by Knaublach and Bennet produced by Granville Barker and Robert Lorraine.

He orders his pilots about in short sharp words of command as though he were the Prisoner of Zenda or the Vicomte de Bragelonne. The mechanics made a swishing noise at their work. The machines all started like clockwork. It was a wonderful production.

That is what Volkoff thinks is witty. What he thinks is l'esprit Parisien. I know a cousin of his very well who is a very clever man much cleverer than Volkoff but who also thinks it clever to say rather acid things. When I asked Volkoff about him Volkoff said "Oh that man!" Which was also characteristic Yes, No?

I quite agree with you that opening a box with an ivory paper cutter is like trying to make Melba sing for nothing. It is like trying to prevent Hillary going away after dinner or cashing a cheque before dinner or asking for a trunk call during dinner. It is like trying to make Evan sacrifice his cigar. It is like trying to make Countess Benckendorff read a letter. It is like trying to stop Conny playing the flute when he is dressing for dinner. It is like trying to make make a Frenchman eat a mincepie. It is like trying to make a German disobey an order. It is like trying to make a Russian keep accounts. It is like trying

  Yours Gildas the son of Caw.

78

Head Quarters, Royal Flying Corps, B.E.F. France.
    27.10.16.
Dear Creirwy,

this afternoon we went to see the new naval Squadron
and very wet and windy it was. In fact a southerly gale blew
all day with great drifts of gusty rain and ragged fluttering
clouds careering across the sky.

We got back about four and at halfpast four just as I was
sitting down to typewrite I noticed that the dark office was
flooded with light so I went out of doors to see what had
happened.

We live at the meeting of five cross roads, and at their
juncture there is a roadside chapel and the roads are bordered
with rows of trees. Now through the trees and over the flat
fields I saw that what had happened was this. The curtain of
storm in the west had been lifted just a little, and underneath
it and behind it there was a sea of liquid light partly pale
gold (the lower part) and partly a luminous sea green, and in
this sea there were low islands and rocks of blazing fire.

But all this was nothing compared to what was happening
in the East. Here the thick grey cloud was turned to purple
by the reflected sunset and right over all of it reaching from
the earth to the zeniths height and then down again to the earth
was the tallest and most perfect rainbow I have ever seen all
incandescent in the glory of the sunset and glistening in the
rain. A marvellous sight. This is the second time I have
described it today in a letter, so much did it strike me.
One seldom sees a perfect rainbow going all the way round
and making an arch over the whole world.

I take it as a symbol of hope victory and peace.
                    Your ruthless,
                        Rubenfresser.

Head Quarters, Royal Flying Corps, B.E.F. France.
    29.10.16.
Dear Rose Aylmer,

yesterday was one of the most tiring days ever devised
for our toil and perplexity. Two Frenchmen came to luncheon
and partook of a Conference.

I got a letter from you from London yesterday written in ink. M. not being yet unpacked. In a little book of poems by J S Squire called Twelve Poems there is one poem called March which I think quite beautiful. Do you know Mr. Squire? Have you any means of of knowing him? Ask Eddy what he is like. He writes to me often and I to him but I have never seen him.

I have read Coriolanus and Timon of Athens by you know who. I think the author must have suffered in his life on account of the ingratitude of friends as nearly all his plays are about ingratitude.

I remain your succinctly,

Giddy Goose.

November 2 1916.

Dear Lady Meyer-Spier-Aspire-higher

Give my best love to your mother. General Seely came today and Mr Massey Prime Minister of New Zealand and Sir Joseph Ward ex Prime Minister of New Zealand. and I called him Sir James and Sir Jacob and Sir Geoffrey and Sir Tristram and Sir Tramtrist and everything except Joseph.

The kind of books I like are indeed memoirs or letters or essays or stories about sailors and adventures or detective or murder stories or stories about swindlers or smugglers or Chinamen in fact anything except novels written by spinsters for spinsters and about passions in the suburbs.

That is all you get from me today.

Your very reverend,

Dean Hole.

3.11.16.

H.Q. R.F.C.

B.E.F. France,

Chere Pastille aux sels naturels,

Seely came to luncheon yesterday and talked nonsense.

He wasted a good deal of our time. When he went away I said it is a pleasure for people to show these things to you because you know what you are looking at. (So little did he know that he wasnt sure which was a stationary engine and which was a rotary) and Seely answered and said : Yes I know everything about it.

I am reading a book called W.O.2. Not about the war office.

There is no chance of my coming for leave before the first of Dec :

Your uralter Wotan.

3.11.16.

Chere Madame Chrysentheme,

> It is misty and the leaves are brown,
> The glass is going down,
> Two late red roses hang upon the tree,
> The motor cyclist skidding in the mud
> Looks upwards at the nimble spad
> Which at a sharp degree
> Is banking and then diving steeply down

The rest is missing.........

Percy Bysshe Evans.

3.1.17.

Head Quarters

Royal Flying Corps

B.E.F. France.

Chere Carbone, (Terme chimique sous lequel on designe le charbon),

I arrived here safely last night after a journey full of unimportant events.

No sooner have I arrived than I find I want

1. A Kalendar for 18 no 1917 from which you can tear off the leaves.

2. An india rubber sponge mine being torn by the rats.

3. The pen Thing gave you. And could you have the stone

81

taken out and a large glass diamond put in its stead? On second thoughts I think not because when you come to No 4 you will see.

4. I want a small wedding present for a Frenchman. That pen would do very well.. *As it is*, if you can spare it; if you cant, will you get me a wedding present for a Frenchman not costing more than than Five pounds or less than four pounds ten shillings. If possible made of gold?

I am going to an Army Conference this morning. The weather here is just as perplexing as it is in England.

Therefore wishing you a happy Epiphany and a prosperous Circumcision

I remain your Charles le Chauvre.

> Head Quarters
> Royal Flying Corps
> B.E.F. France.
> 5.1.17.

Chere Theorie,

which raises the question what is a theory? What is a theory? Is it an etude par raisonnement et deduction d'une science or is it as Harry Cust said to his examiners Une Generalisation centralisatrice? or is it simply une etude basee sur des experiences? Ask Hillary to define a theory. The news is that I have sent my type writer to London in charge of a very good Rugby Football player to have it changed for one of a later type with marginal release and other new gadgets. He will bring back the new one with him.

Today the weather changed from being warm and muggy to being raw and cold. Not exactly raw but rather inclement.

I hope to hear from you tomorrow. I cant get over my joy at the Russian soldiers having at last arrived.

The new Vickers single seater pusher is not a great success. One has no view *down* out of it and the gun is fixed. The Bristol Monoplane has not yet arrived. That is all the news. Who is Lord Corduroy the new Airboard President is he the same as Lord Cawdor and Lord Glamis and will he be King hereafter?

Yrs & Catulle Brandes.

Head Quarters
    Royal Flying Corps
    B.E.F. France.
    6. January 1917. Le Jour des Rois. Twelfth Night or what
    you will.

Rose d'harsoir,
        the beer was bought opposite Victoria station opposite
the Chatham and Dover part at a wine shop whose name I
forget but which might be Foster. It is very difficult to find
if once one misses it but by going slowly back one finds it
finally. Hillary knows exactly where it is. I am delighted
that Rasputin has been killed. If you hear any details let
me know at once. This morning we have a Conference.
Everybody seems to have either a stomachache a cold or a
faceache if you know what that means. In fact everybody feels
queer. None queerer than I do. I enclose a charming picture
of the home and abode of the Muses. As you will see it is
full of poetry.
        The poem about the owl is I believe to be published this
week in the New Witness. Your name is thus committed
to an immortality of fame.
        Only as your surname does not occur in it people will
perhaps think that the owl belonged to Juliet Montagu nee
Capulet.
        Give my love to all or any
                    Your remote El Desdichado.

Head Quarters Royal Flying Corps, B.E.F. France.
    8.1.17.
Face d'or,
        thank you very much for your most interesting letter
received this morning. I enjoyed hearing the details of your
day. Also your news was interesting. Unlike mine. I have
just come in half frozen from a long day in the rain sleet snow
and mud. We visited four Squadrons. You will be grieved
but not surprised to hear that No 15 complain of cracked
cylinders and that No 7 want back wheels for motor cycles.
You will on the other hand be delighted to hear that the Lewis
guns at No 5 fire directly they arrive in a satisfactory way.

In fact they have no complaints. We lost our way on the way back because my servant who was sitting on the box got out and asked a man the way and the man a Frenchman said I suppose a gauche whereas my servant mistranslated gauche as right putting us wrong. The little more and how much it is the little less and what worlds away.

My fingers are still far too cold to type with elegance and accuracy. I am certain your version of the death of Rasputin is correct. Please tell Nathalie from me that I am convinced the Embassy know nothing and if they know it they know it wrong. I have never known an Embassy to be correctly informed about news in my life. The mud is exaggerated just now.

Your chilled to the bone Delorme (Not Marion)

Head Quarters Royal Flying Corps, B.E.F. France.
10.1.17.
Souffleuse de feu,

thank you very much for the Kalendar which arrived this morning and which has on every leaf of it a fresh joke out of Punch. A joke that cheers but does not inebriate. I have little or no news to tell you.

It snowed and rained in the night. It thawed in the afternoon. It is now appreciably warmer. But these changes are very trying as Queen Victoria said about the macaroon biscuits when Prince Beatrice choked.

How are you and what are you doing?
What is the latest gossip?

You see the marginal release enables one to write XXXXXXXXXXX marginal headings or a marginal commentary as Coleridge did in the Ancient Mariner. I will do this next time I write to you.

In the mean time I wish you Good Night.
Your far off Le Roi de la patience.

Civilities.

Remaks on the weather.

Questions.

Valedictory.

84

Head Quarters Royal Flying Corps B E F France. 11.1.17.

The writer addresses Juliet and makes a few remarks on the weather.

O Mai joli,

Thank you for your most interesting letter. It has snowed today and it was indeed cold on the aerodromes. I cannot manage to get warm boots. The warmer they are the colder they get.

The Gold pen and how to deal with it.

With regard to the pen why not send it as you would an ordinary pen in a small box by post and call it Pen one fountain British? In any case send it soon as the Frenchman is to be married shortly. His name is Commandant Pugo.

The writer touches Juliets remark on a sandy beach as one who a long time ago and faraway has had knowledge of such beaches golden in the sun and fringed with surf that softly booms.

How well I understand your wish to lie down on a sandy beach say at Brighton Margate or Broadstairs and here to dream while the motley crowd and the white clad nigger walk past laughing and strumming and munching but you heedless of their coming and going and deaf to their talk and music dream in the sunshine and now and then take up a pebble and drop it once more on the beach.

The writers thoughts turn lightly to Archangel not the Seraph but the Port in the North of Russia.

There the sun shines not in the winter and in the summer the sky grows not dark all the night through but midnight is pale as dawn and lustrous as a pearly sunless noon.

Yes Conny is at Archangel. Therefore you should write to him and send him a book and perhaps an india rubber sponge. But not Russian cigarettes that would be like send Zeppelins to Germany, money to the bank or beauty to Juliet. On the other hand in his ship at Archangel there is no such thing as tea-cosy nor a green parrot nor an American Organ. He is lonely and weighted with heavy responsibilities therfore you would do well to write to him a long letter.

85

The writer bids **Juliet** Adieu fondly.

And now this letter must come to end for all things come to an end even a Lord Mayors dinner followed by speeches and even a Concert at the Queens Hall and even a visit paid in a country house and your youth and mine. Your Tei San.

Head Quarters Royal Flying Corps B E F France.
14.1.17.
Ò magicienne,

it is now imperative you should write to Conny. He was already very lonely and unhappy as it was. Now he will be quite miserable. We had luncheon with General Rawlinson to day. After luncheon we went to a Squadron where the French stunt pilot Flechaire the stunter of stunters flew. There was a thick mist and he couldnt fly higher than about two hundred feet in spite of this he did the tonneau and other stunts. I was thankful when it was over.

Gabriele d'Annunzio has written a book called la Leda senza cigno. I have never seen a Leda without a swan, on the other hand swans without Ledas appear to be quite common. It snowed rather hard last night and it thawed rather hard today. The result was supremely disagreeable. My new Juliet arrives I hope tomorrow.

Your toujours fidele
Mercure (de France).

Head Quarters Royal Flying Corps
B E F France.
16.1.17.
Very important.

The new Juliet has arrived. She is a failure. The letters jam and the alignment is all crooked. I have written to them asking them to send me another and my servant who is on leave will call for it and bring it back but before he does this . . .he comes back on the 23d I want you to go to the shop and

86

to try the machine they propose to send to me and if they demur to convince them with your well known charm.

The shop is the Corona Company 55 Strand. Point out to them that I have been instrumental in getting them distinguished beautiful and illustrious customers. You see how crooked this writes.

It is bitterly cold. Write me any news of the Bencks.

Yours Ali Baba.

Head Quarters Royal Flying Corps. BEF France. 20. 1. 17.
Grand Ange au front d'avoir,

Yesterday someone asked me out to dinner by telephone to dine at the Guest House to meet a Pole (your friend, I suppose). I thought the message came from our Guest House, the Flying Corps Guest House which is in the near vicinity. I said yes meaning no because it is impossible to say no the *first time* by telephone. Then thinking better of it I rang up again to say I was very sorry *but*— The answer came that I had never been asked. I then realised that the message had come from the GHQ Guest House which is 20 miles off. So I rung up the officer in charge of guests to say that I regretted. but. . . . He was out but his subordinate was in and said he would pass on the message. He did, but he sent it to the Commander in Chief. Saying that I regretted that a more important engagement prevented me from accepting his unkind but well-meant invitation.

This I was unaware of till this morning at 8.30 a message came from the GHQ Guest House to know whether I had started as they were still waiting and the Pole was so hungry that he was eating the matches. I tried to answer but I was put into direct communication with Monsieur Briand who was entertaining *guests* at his Guest House. So I rang off. I then tried again and was told that Maurice Guest was out of print and the only copy on loan. However I made a final effort and the answer was that Captain Guest was on leave. Then I gave it up.

There are the advantages of the field telephone in wartime.

I remain yours

Le Veuf, L'Inconsolé.

Head Quarters Royal Flying Corps. B.E.F. France. 22.1.17.
Deilige Fricka,

I have just heard from the Corona Typewriter that they are
sending me a new Juliet. I hope they are doing this through
the medium and channel of 2 A.M. Miller, and not by the
more circuitous post. I shall know the best or the worst
tomorrow. It is appalling living without a Juliet. It is worse
than knocking off smoking. It hampers and paralyses one's
whole life. Please describe me Hilary's evening costume in
greater detail. Does he mean a blue swallow tail coat and
a velvet collar and a Comte d'Orsay tie? or is he dressed in
the more austere mode of John Bright; are his clothes early
Romantic and Byronic or Tory-Democratic or do they savour
of the eighties and le Prince de Galles or the 78 Exhibition,
Mrs. Langtry and Botly Spencer? I had dinner out last in,
in C mess. We had Turkey to eat. One of the members of
this Mess had been sent a lot of Malt Extract by his mother
who thought he was run down so he gave it to the Turkey to eat
and the Turkey became very fat. Last night it was eaten.
The owl poem came out in the *New Witness* but they repeated
one of the lines twice. Why I don't know. Perhaps Hilary
does. Please ask him. How is he? didactic or gentle or world-
weary? It is intensely cold and there are signs of a thaw (not
H. Thaw who has been had up)

Your evanescent
Vacuum-Control.

Headquarters. RFC. BEF. France. 23.1.17.
Idole ennuyeé, in other words Fed-up idol,

this may be the last day I shall be compelled to write
with pen and in ink. I expect 2 AM Miller back today. I
enclose you his letter re the Juliet. You will see how different
this letter—une tranche de vie—is from the letters in
fiction. I have got nothing to smoke. My writing
paper is dwindling. My moustache is frozen; my throat is
sore; my feet are swollen with blains; my joints creak; my
teeth chatter; my hairs fall like leaves in autumn in the suburbs
of Florence say Vallombrosa; so I remain your

Sans Culotte

Head Quarters Royal Flying Corps, B E F.France. 26.1.17.

Chere Peche Melba,

a tragedy of farreaching import happened today. Yesterday we started on the tour of a Brigade including Kiteballoons and incidentally we slept in the coldest house I have ever endured. The water froze while one waited. There was central heating and hotwater pipes but there was no coal and the pipes had burst in the frost being full of cold water. The floors and staircase were made of solid stone. The doors of glass and the windows of fine old cracked glass. The bed rooms which had no fireplaces had not been lived in since the twelfth century and then only by serfs. There was no coal in the house and a very little thin fire wood such as is used by housemaids to lay a fire with. The house stood on the banks of a frozen river in point of fact the Somme. On the other side of the house was a marsh. The ground was covered with frozen snow. The wind cut like a razor. The thermometer registered 14 degrees of frost centigrade and 47 degrees according to something else. Nevertheless I enjoyed the outing. And by drinking enough boiling whisky before going to bed I was sufficiently unconscious to lose sight of the cold. The next day we spent looking at balloons. On our way back and this is the tragedy our luggage fell off the Rolls Royce the G's suitcase made of Willesden canvas containing his razor his new coat his trousers his shoes his favourite buttonhook and an advance copy of the News of the World and my little entout cas bought in St. Petersburg which has been round the world and all over the Balkans twice to Constantinople and through the length and breadth of Russia and the Central Empires. Will you hurry to a chemists or a haircutters and order me

One large shaving brush very large and full a generous one with nothing niggardly about it.

A Gillette razor without blades as I have blades.

An India rubber sponge as before an india rubber nail brush two tooth brushes medium a pair of nail scissors (large) and what is called a cabin holdall made of green canvas to put them in this latter is difficult and cant be bought at a chemists but can be bought at any Army Equipment shop or at the Stores. If the latter is too difficult leave it.

Your loving Pair et Impair. Rouge couleur.

Head Quarters Royal Flying Corps, B.E.F. France.
    27.1.17.
O venusta Sirmio,

    this is the last sheet of my last block. It is to be
expended in a letter to you. Everybody here likes this big
Roman type better than the more measly pica. What do you
think. I think it is bold and beautiful. Among the rest of
my luggage I also lost a buttonhook. Please put up a candle
to St. Anthony for me and if he finds it he shall have a whole
heap. Today the wind is in the East and very strong so it is
still cold but I believe it is not really so cold as it was yesterday
although at first touch it feels colder. Talking of the difficulty
of providing me with books remember that I have a passion
for all Rider Haggards books and I have not read nearly all of
them. I lately read the Holy Flower and the Ivory Child and
I found them both admirable. I have also a passion for Max
Pembertons books. I have just read one called the Red Morn
which I enjoyed very much. I here pause to warm my figures
which are as cold as those of the dawn. But it has proved in
vain so I continue with cold fingers. Please do not forget to
send me a detailed portrait of your new hat. But I suppose by
this time you have got a still newer hat.
                    Yours exceedingly faithful
                            Achates.

Head Quarters Royal Flying Corps B E F France.
    27.1.17.
Dulce Loquens,

    I do not think that Lipkins cigarettes in any way resemble
Russian or any other kind of cigarettes. I find them detestable.
On the other hand I can smoke the little ones from Freiburg
with pleasure.

    2. In choosing a book remember that I by no means want
insist on a good book. I can read all books that are very bad
if bad enough. I can read all detective stories all without
exception. What I dont like is the mediocre. The ordinary
good novel I abhor.

    I loathe Edith Whartons books all of them. She is the
author I hate most.

Do not mix up Marie Corelli and Hall Caine.   Hillary will explain to you the vast difference between them.

Marie Corelli is much better than Hall Caine.

XXXXXXXXX Send me just any bad book that looks enter-taining or exciting.

Let it be written by a man if possible and not by a Bint unless it is a detective story.   Bints do that very well indeed.

I remain your smouldering volcano,

E. Tna.

Head Quarters Royal Flying Corps, B E F France.

29.1.17.

Joli Rayon de soleil,

I dont believe I wrote to you yesterday as I was out all day but of that more anon.   First and most important I hope you ordered me a shaving brush whether you received my order countermanding the first order or not because last night owing to the intense cold my shaving brush burst the ivory part that is to say and all the hairs which are badgers hairs are coming out and this adds to the difficulty of shaving and the acerbity of life.   Secondly how extraordinary is the passion of Bints for the colour of magenta but to go so far as to get a magenta ribbon is to go too far.   I beg of you to have it exchanged at once for a blue ribbon or a black ribbon be dignified or eccentric but dont be mediocre.   A magenta ribbon is mediocre and paltry.   Yesterday I drove through the freezing air to Amiens to pick up four Russian Flying Corps officers who came here on a visit.   At Amiens I met Reggie Cooper and we had luncheon at the Restaurant Gobert.   Oysters to begin with then eggs pointes d'asperges not oeufs brouilles then langouste then canard sauvage all hot and delicious.   Then we went to the station and met the Russian officers and took them home with us to dinner.   One of them was charming they were all intensely friendly natural and fussless directly.   After dinner we all played Tziganne songs.   The cold wave continues.   I have not much further to add except that I am reading a very old book by Henry James with pleasure.   It is called the Portrait of a Lady.

I remain yours Plutus the Plutocrat.

Head Quarters Royal Flying Corps,
      B.E.F. France.
      31.1.17.
Enfant de pure joie,

       Two letters arrived from you to me this morning both
of them written in magenta. Please change that ribbon at
an early opportunity. It offends all my five senses my heart
my brain my soul my body. Get a blue one or a black one
or a green one anything but magenta. With regard to changing your house I have two things to point out. Firstly if you
live in a less central neighbourhood you will find the difficulties
of communication transport and transit irksome and difficult.

       Secondly house moving in wartime and in winter is a
terrible business.

       Thirdly   if you give up your house you may very likely
regret it. Houses are not very easy to find and a house that
is not after you taste will have a depressing effect on your
morale.

       Fourthly consider carefully whether it would really be true
and not a false economy. Were you to take a new house you
would certianly spend on the doing up of it more than a years
rent of your present house. Ponder over all these things. You
might buy a barge and live on the Thames when it thaws that
is to say.

       It has been a very cold day. I have been out at 2nd A D.
I dont think the last captured machine was an Albatross because
it has V shaped struts and a radiator on the centre section and
not on the sides as in the Albatross Scout. I think it is the
machine hitherto called Halberstadt. Even that may be a mis-
nomer. Have you ever been to Halberstadt? I have.

       It is the Harz country.
              Yours truly,
                 Inigo Thornton-Smith.

Head Quarters Royal Flying Corps, B.E.F. France.
1.2.17.
Mer miroitante,

       I regret to say that I have not received a letter from
you today. Neither from you nor from anyone else. The post

came indeed but to me it brought nothing. Neither parcel nor letter nor circular nor bill nor postcard nor advertisement nor a demand for a subscription nor a scrap of paper. Please do not let this happen again. I am reading in my spare moments Allan Quatermain by Rider Haggard. The weather prophet prohesies a thaw as it has become very much warmer and the snow has begun to melt he is not risking very much but he may be wrong after all. The G. has got a new pair of boots. Gordon is going home to take charge of a machine gun school. Brancker is staying here. He had read my poem about your owl not in the *New Witness* but he had seen a typewritten copy. How did this occur? Please ask Hillary whether the line which was printed twice running in the poem was printed like that on purpose or whether it was a mistake. The G. has invited Belloc to stay here and the invitation has been sanctioned and approved and stimulated by the Commander in Chief who wants to see him too and who will ask him to luncheon. It hope he will come soon. Have you invested in the war loan? I have. My shaving brush never recovered from the great frost. It remained permanently fletri. It had to be shot. This was thought to be the kindest solution. We tried rubbing it with snow but this only made it regain a partial consciousness and awake to terrible and needless suffering so a merciful bullet (sparklet mark 3) put an end to its long and useful career. It was buried in the dustheap. I was asked to dinner to meet Bernard Shaw last night but the inclement weather prevented me from going.

I remain
Your inseparable,
Lawrence the licentious.

Head Quarters Royal Flying Corps,
    B.E.F. France.
    2.2.17.
Tête soyeuse,

    I heard from you last night. Something happened to the post and it came unexpectedly like a thief in the daytime. It is much colder than it has ever been. The Junior Army and Navy Stores, instead of sending me what Pockney

ordered with discrimination, send me an invoice and say if I
will send them a cheque they will send me the things. They
will be punished for want of trust sense and alacrity because
I no longer want the things and I shall write and tell them.

I will tell you that I might have gone to Petrograd. They
wanted me to go and I was sorely tempted to for at least twenty
four hours.

Then I took the wish and plucked it out of my heart.

Entbehren sollst du entbehren.

As the German Emperor remarked to the German Empress
one day when he refused to pay her bills.

Yours Rollicking,

Little Lord Fauntleroy

Head Quarters Royal Flying Corps, B.E.F. France.

4.2.17.

Pobre barquilla mia,

yesterday no boat arrived so the result is we had no letters either yesterday or today. You can imagine the effect this had on my spirits. Not even a letter in magenta.

The weather is cold and sunless. The glass is going down. The weather prophet thinks it may thaw in time.

Last night an Italian officer arrived to stay the night. He spoke English with a perfect accent but laboriously.

A charming Frenchman Commandant DuPeuty of the French Flying Corps came to luncheon and after luncheon Commandant Pugo arrived par la voie des airs in a Horrace. A Horrace is a mixture between a Henry Farman and a Morris Farman.

Margin notes:

EXHORTATION IN SPANISH

NO POST. NOT EVEN A MAGENTA.

WEATHER COLD AS HELL
THEY SAY

GUESTS AT HQ RFC

FRENCH AND A DAGO.

HENRY-MORRIS MACHINES COMBINED MAKE ONE HORRACE.

The Italian officer had no sense of humour. He was painstaking but heavy in hand and desirous of receiving and imparting useful information. He took an Intelligent interest in eveything and said he drank water to keep up the good reputation his countrymen had for sobriety. To which I answered that I drank wine and *rum* to maintain the bad reputation my countrymen had for inebriety. He was pained and puzzled.

DAGO A DARNED BORE.

DAGO ON WATERWAGON.

STAFF CAPTAIN SHOCKS DAGO.

I am very anxious to hear the news from London. What are the Americans going to do and what does Sir George Alexander think of the political situation?

NEWS. STAFF CAPTAIN SAYS YOU CAN SEARCH ME FOR.

WHAT DOES GEORGE THINK? NOT LOYDIE

FRENCH BOOK SOME BOOK.

Coutelines latest book Coco Coco & Tata is amusing. Yr. E. Mu.

Head Quarters Royal Flying Corps B.E.F. France.

O mas dura que marmol a mis que jas.

Captain addresses Juliet. CALLS HER DANDY NAMES

I received a letter from you last night but a very short one. As the Spring or rather the winter progresses so do your letters get shorter and shorter even as the days get longer and longer. Please let this situation be changed.

JULIET SKIMPS BILLETS DAYS LONGER LETTERS SHORTER.

To-day it is snowing hard. That is all I shall say about the weather.

BLIZZARD BLOCKS BOULOGNE.

A man dined here last night who told us all about the habits of beavers and how roast beaver was better than roast mutton. This I can well believe.

ROAST BEAVER MAKES MUTTON LOOK LIKE 30 CENTS.

95

CURIOUS CONDUCT OF
CABOTIN.

-

CHARACTERISTIC
CAPTAIN SAYS

TOWN TALK WHAT IS IT?

FAREWELL CAPTAIN SAYS
ASKS FOR MORE
COPY LESS MAGENTA.

Another man dined here last night who told me that when a machine caught fire the other day Major Cabotin said to the crowd stand back. He then borrowed a cigarette walked up to the blazing machine and lit his cigarette at it. Isnt this typical?

I should like to hear the talk of the town with regard to the attitude conduct and état dame of America and its consequences.

Farewell and please write me longer letters in future and of a more personal kind and if possible not in magenta but in some nobler colour and less offensive.

Yours raucous,
Booze fighter.

Headquarters Royal Flying Corps,
6. 2. 17.
My Dear,

I am desperately sorry to hear your mother is worse. I trust they will be able to prevent her suffering. It is terrible Dear Ju, one blow after another and battalions of sorrows.

I enclose you a photograph of Bron the last one ever done.

Bless you my child,
Yours M.

Head Quarters Royal Flying Corps,
8. 2. 17.
Celestial anhelo,

Juliet appears to be drunk. As to the cold it is colder. The clock in this room struck 256 yesterday and nobody knew how to stop it. It is now being mended. Yesterday afternoon I drove into Boulogne and whilst there I bought a whiting and

96

a herring. I am just going out for the day. The wind is blowing straight from the mountains and the immeasurable plains. This morning my toothpowder was frozen into a pink topaz. Nan sent me a book called the XXXX Just Men of Cordova which I enjoyed very much. Philip Sassoon recommended me a book which he said was excellent. I ordered it got it read it and think it without exception the worst and the coarsest book I have ever read in my life besides being crude melodramatic dull ill-written and falsely rustic.

Your affectionate friend,
Don Dinero.

Head Quarters Royal Flying Corps,
9.2.17.

Ensueno de suavisima ternura,

CAPTAIN
COVERED
WITH BLAINS.

My chilblain is causing me acute pain. Last night I put some ointment on it recommended by a chemist. It burnt the flesh and kept me awake all night. All day long the sun has shone on the hard white fields and the brown bare trees. The sky has been like silver the earth like a white altar. The beauty of the landscape was marred by a North East wind.

WINTRY
WEATHER
IN FRANCE.

Last night at dinner I said to my neighbour

" The man then said "

MAURICE
MAKES
A BON MOT.

The G. overheard me and said XXXXXXX Is it me you are alluding to as the man? I said "No, Sir, I allude to you as the Superman".

How badly we type in the cold weather.

TYPE WRITING
DUD
IN FROST.

I have got heaps of books. Now. I am reading A London Life by Henry James.

VALE

Your true Frascati.

Head Quarters Royal Flying Corps. B.E.F. France.
10. 2. 17.
Flor deliciosa,
Lord Cavanagh had luncheon here today. Who knows who may dine here to-night? Have you invested in the war loan? I have in two separate banks. I wrote to one bank and said will you lend me all your capital and invest it in the war loan? I sometimes wonder why the banks cant invest the money straight instead of lending it to us to invest. But no doubt that is against the principles of economics. The gold pen has arrived. Also the cabin holdall and the shaving of Shagpat and the indiarubber nail-brush. Although my luggage was found I am very glad to have these pieces de rechange. One never knows.
Your memorable Don Nicomedes Pastor Diaz.

13. 2. 17.
Head Quarters Royal Flying Corps, B.E.F. France.
Tu dulce majestad,
A tragedy has just been averted or rather a drama, one of those episodes that so rarely happen in real life. I very nearly . . . but no why should distress you unnecessarily since the error was averted.
Tomorrow will be Saint Valentines Day.
My birthday is in April on the 27th. If you would like to give me a birthday present this is what I should like. One piece of red sealing wax, a long piece and a seal with a cryptic inscription or motto on it in a foreign tongue or english something beautiful and full of hidden meaning.
I am giving you plenty of warning and if you will tell me when your birthday is and what you would like as a birthday present I will take the necessary steps.
Hillary arrives here tomorrow. I am looking forward to his visit. It is thawing so I don't think the glacial period is upon us yet. On the contrary I prophesy a hot a very hot summer.
I hope your headache is better.
My chilblain is much better.
Your with respect Manuel Maria de Arjona.

Head Quarters Royal Flying Corps,
B.E.F. France.

14. 2. 17.

I address you thus :

H.B. 2. J.D. B.U.T.

But I am not very good at typewriting nor for that matter at any kind of writing and least of all at letterwriting so I hand Juliet over to Maurice.

Hillary as you see is not expert with the machine as you and I. I having already written to you once today have nothing more to say to you except to assure you once more of my regard and my consideration.

This letter although it looks short took a long time to write as it took Hillary half an hour to write those three lines which are written in red.

We remain,
Yours obedient Servants,
M. Baring,
H.B.X.M.P.2.J.D.B.U.T.

P.S. Maurice is a liar ! A bad one too ! For I not only wrote in prose but in verse : and good verse too !

"Judith for triumph ; Miriam for regret ;
For frailty Eve ; for beauty Juliet
For beauty and for beauty, Juliet ; yes !
Juliet for all-consuming loveliness ! "

Head Quarters Royal Flying Corps, B.E.F. France
15. 2. 17.
Dear Rosalba,

I have got a sore throat and a pain in my head. Hillaire is here. He arrived yesterday without his fur coat unless it had fur inside it unbeknownest to me. He goes to Paris to morrow and thence to Lyons and England.

The shaving brush arrived this morning. It is an amour of a shaving brush, simple et naturelle et timide sans embarras.

I feel in too small health to write at greater length.

Yr devoted
W. D. and H. O. Wills.

16.2.17.   Head Quarters RFC.
Chere Poine d'Argentan,

Hillarys visit has been a great success.   He left this afternoon for Amiens en route for Lyons where he is to lecture.

The G. sent for Louis who was at the trenches and he dined and slept last night.   He liked him and thought him intelligent.

Today we had luncheon with the Field Marshal..   Hillary was very dignified and civil.

I have got a sore throat.
It is indeed no better.

World wearynes complains
of
so
are we all.
Maurice says.

I feel exceedingly tired.   Hillary looked and was very tired too.

We are all tired.   The world is tired of the past Oh might it sink and rest at last.

Yours truly,
Percy Bysshe
Harmsworth-Yousoupoff-Elston.

Head Quarters Royal Flying Corps, B.E.F. France.
17.2.17.

Dear Gold Flake,

it is thawing hard.   The thaw is mixed with a slight drizzle. It is foggy as well.   Mists rise and drift northwards from the valley of the Somme.

This morning there was an investiture and a review.

So dense was the fog that the army was invisible and seemed like an army of ghosts marching past to

phantom pipes and an unearthly Marseillaise.   The G. was decorated with the XXXXXXXXX Croix of Comm[an]deur de la Legion d'honneur.

I was decorated with nothing.

The French Commander in Chief General Nivelle pinned on the decorations himself and kissed the Major Generals.

The ceremony lasted an hour and

a half.

Then we all went home.

Yr & Marcus Ordeyne.

Head Quarters Royal Flying Corps, B.E.F. France.
18.2.17.

Dear Vesta (Swan not Tilley),

Thaw
thickens   SOME
on Somme   THAW.
Blind
Bat
invades
Bedroom.

It has been thawing violently. Out of the thaw a mist has arisen. Last night or rather the night before last a bat came into my bedroom in the middle of the night. It was as blind as a bat. So much so that I had to light a candle and throw field boots at it till it flew out again. I had always thought bats were blind in the daytime but could see at night. They cant.

The fire has gone out. The post is interrupted so you may not get this letter for weeks. We have had no letters for three days. Nor newspapers but parcels. I have received

two. One containing cigarettes and the other a book of reminiscences. I have already read part of the book and smoked some of the cigarettes.

That is all for the present.

Yours Le gendre de Monsieur.

Head Quarters Royal Flying Corps, B.E.F. France.
20.2.17.
My Dear Grecian Urn,
I have had a most exhausting day. I have been to luncheon with a French General. You will perhaps guess who it was when I tell you that if you think of the French for level you will arrive at the first syllable of his name. If you think of the French for She you will perhaps guess the second syllable of his name.

His anteroom or antichambre was heated to fever heat. We waited standing a long time while various ADCs flitted in and out of the room. The a v nice sub-General came in and made conversation and was pleasant. Then an A D C came and whispered to me where I was to sit at table. Then suddenly the General came in from an unexpected door and said How do you do naturally and with energy but did not break my fingers in the saying of it.

Then another door was thrown open and a white jacketed soldier said that the General was served and in we went. I sat next to the other General.

I forgot to tell you a lame Minister was also present. The G. sat on the Generals left and the Minister on his right. the menu was as follows.

Filets soles a la Juliette Duff
Boeuf demode
Pate de foi maigre
Crepes a la Crepy
Plum Duff a la Juliet
Plum Pudding.

The General asked whether I talked French
I said Oui Mon General, comme une vache espagnole.
After luncheon we proceeded to business and then we drove home, I exhausted and I have been writing ever since about the results of our visit so have little or no time to write to you.

We all feel tired to death. We are not enjoying the war. We wish it would end. We consider it is waste of time and great waste of money.

Your remarkable,
Stephen Remarx.

Head Quarters Royal Flying Corps B E F France.
21.2.17.

Dear Lady Caroline Lamb,

The seal question.

I want a seal that is not jocose. On the other hand it need not be over serious.

I should not like the inscription to be either in Hebrew or Sanscrit.

I should never the less like it to be enigmatic. Something which should at the same time arrest stimulate and attract the mind without baffling it. Or rather though it may baffle it should not confuse nor perplex. Mona Lisa smile although palpable is baffling. I should like the inscription to be like Mona Lisas smile.

I should like it to be in English French Latin Greek Spanish Italian Russian or Maori but not in Danish Swedish Polish Portuguese Dutch Flemish German or Japanese.

And, on the whole not in Chinese.

Writing letters.

Sugar in tea. Z (He doesnt like it)

Sausages for breakfast (They are unobtainable)

Queens Hall concerts.

A box at the opera.

I subsequently nobbled the coat was fur lined.

Although the lining is not thick.

I disagree with your diagnosis.

Hudson was an artist. But he hadnt quite enough physical force and stamina to balance the creative fire in him. He was never in love with his cousin. He died of home truths said to him by his friend.

And I remain,
Yours woeful
Pallas's sand Grouse.

Margin notes:

SHOULD SEAL FOR BIRTHDAY SHOULD INTIGUE BUT NOT CONFUSE

LENT
WHAT SHALL CAPTAIN RENOUNCE. INK?

food favourite music. favorita.

Belloc
in
Furs.

RODERICK HUDSON.
BINT
NOT SO MUCH TO BLAME.

RODERICK HAD NO USE FOR PLAIN COUSIN.

Head Quarters Royal Flying Corps, B E F France.
22.2.17.
Sonorosa llama,

the most important piece of news is this that I **may** be coming to England for 48 or even for 60 hours. The date of departure is changed daily and depends on the fog the tides the mines the submarines and the health of Lord Cowdray.

But, 1 may arrive on Monday or Tuesday possibly Wednesday.

Yr Orpheus the Morpheus

Head Quarters Royal Flying Corps B E F France.
6.3.17.
Madame la Marechale (Niel),

Today I spoke with a Russian prisoner who had escaped from the German lines. He was 22 but looked 16. He had been starved. Today the weather was springlike.

The snow has melted. The first message of Spring was whispered to day to the weary earth.

It was well received.

We are all weary of winter,
we are all weary of war,
I cut my hand with a splinter
So I cannot write any more.

Your ruthless Ricky.

Head Quarters R F C B E F FRance.
7.3.17. .
Adorable adorée.

the winds of March are blowing and the clouds of March are snowing
    and the grass of March is growing
        and the wind is cold
    and your faithful bard,
        so feeble and so old
    takes it hard,
    (takes what hard? why all that . . . .)

I have no news for you except that the barometer is very low.

This letter you will perceive is entirely about the weather.

I have seriously curtailed my smoking. Today I have smoked no cigarettes yesterday only four.

On the other hand I am longing to chew some gum.

Your &
Ben Gun.

Head Quarters Royal Flying Corps, B E F France.
    8.3.17.

Chere Bourgeoise (veau à la),

I have read two more books by Henry James. One called The Other House which is like a quiet subtle thrilling play and another called The Tragic Muse which I tried and failed to read twenty years ago and which I have now read with greedy delight.

How strange are the vicissitudes of taste.

I shall go on reading Henry James till I have read all his books.

It needs a European war to make one find out some things.

Mite caput (Yours)
Fier Sicambre.

    9.March 18 No 19 17.

Head Quarters Royal Flying Corps, B E F France.

Casta Neaera,

    the giboulees continue mingled with a high wind. The cook at the fifth Brigade applied to go home for a few days leave because he said he had already some beautiful daughters and would like a little son. His motive was thought patriotic and his request will accordingly be granted.

So saying the weary writer laid down his type writer and sighing deeply twitched his mantle blue,

Tomorrow to fresh woods and G H Q.

Your affectionate,
Miser Catullus.

Head Quarters
  Royal Flying Corps,
    10.3 17.
Sol. degli occhi miei,
  it thawed in the night and this caused me to wake up
like Mr Beit and to scream in the night.
  You say you are to have the fullness taken out of your
skirts because you have had wind from Paris that the Paris
Bints are contemplating such action.
  I heartily commend you intention. Always be ahead of the
fashion appear to lead it even if you are following it. Do
not be fashions slave.
  No, I dont think we shall have the breadth taken out of
our coats although we may have the wind taken out of our
sails.
  Fashion in the army is set differently according to the
different arms. The cavalry have one fashion and the Infantry
another. The cavalry is the more daring and elastic they have
lots of breadth in their coats and they wear imaginative ties.
  The Guards go in for fit in contradistinction to fancy and
the R F C are various some being dressy and some not.
  I am longing for an acid drop or a piece of barley sugar.
I have quite given up smokimg cigarettes.
  And you?
                              Yours most anxiously,
                                    Buridan.

    Head Quarters
      R F C B E F France.
        11. 3. 17.
Abeille dorée,
  I have just come home. It has been a Spring day. It
began with a slight shower. Then it cleared and the air became
soft and the sky soft and grey with fitful glimpses of sunshine.
  We drove along the muddy roads till we came to the ancient
city where the young Queen died of a broken heart and the
old King died of a broken foot, and there we had luncheon
in an apartment. After an hour's discussion of important
matters with the French Aviation Commanders.

At luncheon we had hors d oeuvres turkey potatoes salsifis
saldà de chocorée, all delicious.
Then we drove home and the drive·took three hours and
a half as the crow flies.
And here I am at home writing to you.
That being so,
I remain,
Your restless
Jean Sans Terre.

Head Quarters
Royal Flying Corps,
B.E.F.France.
Dulcis Ipsithilla,
Beware of the Ides of March. Beware also of the March
winds and the March fogs and the March hares and March
dogs. They are all in full swing at the present moment.
All of them are disagreeable too.
Yesterday was one of the most exhausting days on record.
It rained all day. We inspected a depot. An aircraft depot.
You little know what that means.
Today it is foggy.
Arent you pleased that Bagdad has been taken?
When I was a lad at Bagdad,
Hillary will finish the poem for you.
The sun is not shining. Please write me thé news.
The chickens are whining. And so are the Jews.
Your serviceable
Beardmore 160.

Head Quarters
Royal Flying Corps,
B.E.F. France.
18.3. 17.
Mas festiva que las auras,
I forgot to tell you that there is another cheap edition
of some of the long short-stories of Henry James published

107

in small convenient separate volumes and costing two shillings each. The publishers name is Martin not Luther but Secker. He also publishes the poems of Flecker.

> The poems of Flecker
> Are published by Secker.

I have entirely stopped smoking. I dont know whether I shall ever take to it again. I have no chewing gum. But I have just finished an orange drop. With regard to the footman in the R F C. At present all people like footmen are being combed out and taught to make planes or some other useful trade so it will be difficult if not impossible to comb him in if that is to say he is class A man. If however he is a class B man or suffers from flat feet consumption epilepsy or peritonitis it will be quite easy. So you had better tell me if he is Class A or Class B.

> I remain your well disposed,
> T. Shandy.

> Head Quarters
> Royal Flying Corps,
> B.E.F. France.
> 20.3. 17.

Ma commere,

I am glad the seal has arrived although three weeks too soon for your birthday. The inscription on it is written in Spanish. It means

> Plutot morte que differente,

Antes muerta que mudada, as I daresay someone has already told you by now. The weather has been tempestuous and the roads are very bad.

The Emperor of Russia should have remembered as we warned him the Ides of March a day fatal to Emperors. I wonder whether he will come to England and live near Richmond.

Les Rois s'en vont mais les Rois reviennent.
Such is the philosophy of your
> restive,
> George Rostrevor.

Head Quarters
   Royal Flying Corps,
      22. 3. 17.
Felicité parfaite,
      It doesnt mean I would sooner die than change . . .
[my mind or my hat] but sooner die than *be* changed ie be
different or otherwise. In other words Io sono Io as Nora said
when played in Italian by Eleonora Duse.
      It is as perhaps you have by now perceived a flattering
motto. . Your seal has not yet arrived but the chewing gum
has and is being chewed. What an addtion to life is chewing
gum. It has many advantages over smoking. You can chew
in Church and at the play. You can chew by night you can
chew by day. You can chew when walking or riding or talking
you can chew at the Zoo. Vers libres. Or petit poeme en
prose.
      I am overjoyed by the events in Russia. Pourvu que cela
dure as Napoleons mother kept on saying. I know nearly
all the peoples implicated.
                    YRS.% D. Gummed.

      Head Quarters, R.F.C.
         B.E.F. France.
Tu la luna en las sombras argentas,
      thank you very much for yesterdays letter which had
a little bit of just the kind of news I like to hear. The kind
which the newspapers never mention. Brancker arrived last
night.   D. Henderson is arriving today.
      So much for arrivals. No, I forgot the Barley Sugar arrived
yesterday at noon. His arrival was greeted by an ovation.
      I am not sure chewing gum didnt give me indigestion
yesterday. Please ask a good doctor whether it does or not.
That is a thing we must know, as it is of no use to give up
one pernicious habit if we immediately replace it by one still
more pernicious, and I would rather oversmoke than over-
indigest. Please find out about this witthout fail, You who live
in a nest of doctors.
                  Your optimistic,
                     Op. 1.

Head Quarters
    Royal Flying Corps,   24. 3. 17.
Belle au Bois de Boulogne,

      Yesterday I went to Boulogne to fetch D Henderson and I took the opportunity of going to the dentist. He was an English dentist who has the reputation of being the best dentist in Paris. He is now doing his bit. But it. is a very different thing to go to a good dentist in war time and to a good dentist in peace time. In peace time the good dentist is very careful to hurt you as little as possible ; in stopping a tooth he makes the hole very gradually using a whole series of files and drills one finer than the other and growing fine by degrees and gradually less and his conduct of the steel spike is nice. He says "A little tender there?" or "Hold up your hand directly I hurt you." he knows well if he does hurt you he will lose your valuable custom. In war time how different.

      Seizing hold of your head he inserts a broad drill into your tooth and goes on boring a hole with all his force till the hole is made. No matter how much you struggle and scream and kick. I did all three but it was no good holding my head in a vice he dug the drill deeper and deeper into the tender tooth till the hole was finished. Of course instead of taking half an hour it only took a few minutes and that when it is over is an

      I wonder what I was going to say an advantage perhaps.

      Today the March winds have been blowing like Billy Ho and werent they cold. Not Arf. And werent the roads bad Not Arf. And werent the aerodromes drafty not arf.

      I saw the machine that had been flown by and captured from Prince Frederick Charles of Prussia son or grandson of the Red Fox or the Red Duke or the Red Robe I forget which He is wounded and is going well. The first words he uttered were How is Lady Juliet Duff?

      I dont know why I am writing you such a long letter Perhaps in the hope of getting a long one back.

      Hope springs eternal in the human breast
               of
                  Your affect
                    Hope Less.

Head Quarters Royal Flying Corps,
    B.E.F. France. 25.3.17.
Femme aux yeux d'or,
        thank you very much for the scrap of paper you sent
me last night. You promised a long letter. I visited the
3rd Brigade today with General David Henderson but I did
not propose luncheon with the General Commanding as I
thought he was in quarantine for German measles. It now
turns out he is out of quarantine and very huffy. So I have
caused a catastrophe. It is most unfortunate.
                    Yours wistfully
                        U.M. Brella.

        Head Quarters
        Royal Flying Corps,
            B.E.F. France.
            26.3. 17.
Triste larme d'argent,
        The wind has been blowing very coldly today
        That is almost all I have got to say.
        General David Henderson leaves tomorrow
        With a book in his luggage by Lord George Borrow
        Who was not a lord but the rhythms require
        That I for once should become a liar.
        Basil Blackwood who *is* a Lord,
            Put away his saddle and sword
        Last night and dined at our friendly table,
            and stayed as long as he was able,
        Today he returns to a trench near the Somme
                                (pronunced sum)
        With a piece of American chewing gum
            From my ample store;
            Should he want some more,
            I will send it by letter post
            (But registered lest it be lost,)
            My rhymes run dry
            So I say Good bye,
                Sleep well,
            Farewell. Always your Bernard Shore.

Head Quarters
Royal Flying Corps,
B.E.F. France.
27.3.17.

Caraissima Gazza ladra,

many thanks for yours of yesterday. As to the seal I think a seal in hand is worth two in the shop. I should rather have a seal which was a topaz and looked like a cairngorm than a seal which was a cairngorm and looked like a topaz. But the three sided seal sounds very nice. I leave the matter to you. I have great confidence in your taste choice and knowledge of the human heart. You ask me if I should think the same of you if you were to become dowdy and ill dressed. Of course I should not. My affection would at once cool. I should feel quite differently towards you. One touch of Sloane Street in your clothes and half my affection would die.

Of course if it were only pretence, if while pretending no longer to bother nor to buy you were in reality having ultra simple but ultra chic clothes made by an obscure sempstress in Bloomsbury I should not only approve but applaud.

My affection would rise in soaring spirals. David went away this morning. I think he enjoyed himself and that his visit did him good.

It snowed again last night. What do you hear of Russia?

Yours truly
Gabriel Junks.

Head Quarters
Royal Flying Corps,
B.E.F. France.

Sehr Geehrte Kundry,

I agree with you about these post mortem examinations which are of such frequent occurrence. They have added a new terror to death.

I loathe analytic memorials especially when they are pompous. They are so fearfully untrue to nature. They leave out all the essential and they have an air of funeral crape about them or else a strained and false naturalness.

In future I think I shall write to you entirely in Latin. It is more dignified as we neither of us know Chinese well enough to write it.

Yr loving Gondicarius.

Head Quarters R. F. C.
B.E.F. France.
31. 3. 17.

Goddess of shades, and Huntress, who at will
Walkst on the rolling sphere, and through the deep,
On thy third reign, the Earth, look now, and tell
What soap, what kind of soap thou biddst me use,
What fragrant soap, that I may wash myself
Each day, with water warm, and spotless towels.
What seal, what seal of stone I may expect;
Sapphire or topaz or chalcedony,
Or lucky chrysoprase or emerald,
Or darkling opal from Australia;
Engraved with what delightful epigraph,
In solid English or perspicuous French,
Or lofty Latin or more plastic Greek;
What rhyme allusive or what perfect prose
Or haply but one pregnant word, one phrase
Elliptic, or a single syllable
Chargéd with significance, or feathery-winged
With attic wit; in any case secure
Of audience and comprehension.
Sweet Cynosure of Brook Street, fare you well,
Your most obedient faithful Abdiel.

Head Quarters
Royal Flying Corps,
B.E.F. France.
1.4. 17.

Sweet Queen of Parley, daughter of the Illustrated London News, (the above literary allusion will not be detected by you unless you invoke the aid of a scholar, I suggest E Marsh)

As to the seal, I am very glad it shall have three faces. The
Seal with three faces is a good name. I am glad it is made
of Cairngorm. I am glad it will have two mottoes but they
must not be in the same language.

With regard to the library, I should advise you to be a
Life Member, if the Life membership is not too expensive.

I am very fond of the London Library. It is one of my
favourite haunts in London.

> Yes I am longing for the graven seal;
> I hope that haply fauns with cloven heel
> will not be absent and I also hope
> The image will be sanctioned by the Pope,
> I trust the superscription will be fit
> > At cur nitor in arduum?
> > I remain
> > > Your
> > > > tantae pulchritudinis amator,
> > > > Pithy Ass.

Head Quarters Royal Flying Corps, B.E.F. France.
2. 4. 17.

Spring of Bandusia.

> Red wine and festal garlands are thy meed.
> Tomorrow I shall offer thee a kid;
> His waxing brow, his budding horns, prophetic
> are ready for the war that goes with love,
> But all in vain; the blood of this wild offspring
> Thine icy waters must incarnadine.

> The dogstar and the incandescent days
> Can parch thee not, and weary of the plough,
> the oxen, and the silly sheep astray
> Shall find in thee delicious, cool retreat.

> Thou shalt be numbered amongst famous springs,
> The rocks, the ilex, whence thy ripples fall
> Tinkling, shall live forever in my verse.
> > Yours very truly,
> > Corporal Bates.

3. 4.17.
H.Q. R.F.C.
Dark veiled Cotytto,
    this is most alarming for two days I have had no letter from you. Two days running. The Boches have cut down every rose tree in the country they abandoned and spoiled every chair with a redhot poker. This cannot have been a military necessity. From a military point of view it must have been great waste of time.
    Please write to me soon without fail.
Your in some respects
star-led wizard.
Cyriack Skinner.

Easter Sunday 1917.
April 8. QOQU or in other words 1917.
Sara, belle d'indolençe,
    today as you see is Easter Sunday. I wonder where you are spending the festival whether in London or in the country. I did not hear from you yesterday. Your letters become rarer and fewer and further between. It froze last night. Are you glad that the Americans are at war against the Huns and not with them. This cannot by any stretch of imagination be regarded as a triumph for German Diplomacy. What do you think? Please write to me when you have time if you have not forgotten my name and direction. The latter is Head Quarters Royal Flying Corps the same as it was last year and the year before and the former is
Charles de Charolais.

Head Quarters
Royal Flying Corps,
B.E.F. France.
Chere Arlequinine,
    at last I heard from you. Yes the records arrived as I have already announced to you. It is still cold but not freezing yesterday the G. and I went by air to eleven different

Squadrons. It was very cold in the air. I broke the elastic of my goggles at once and this made it much sorer for the eyes. Did you see a poem by Hillary in the New Statesman called Hannaker Mill? It is most beautiful. The best poem, I think, he has ever written. I am trying to learn how to smoke now but I find it is nauseous. How could one ever have liked it? Do you think that like Macbeth I shall smoke no more that I shall be deprived of the utieshenie zhisni? How rash it is ever to give up anything except a railway ticket.

I am now in the painful situation of having forgotten how to smoke and not having learnt how to chew.

Let my example be a warning to you and never give up smoking.

The state of Wisconsin is pro Merg because thousands of Mergs live there. But a lot of Poles live there too. The Poles do not like the Germans nor are the Germans fond of the Poles.

I received a very nice Easter Egg on Easter Day full of chocolate and tied up with a ribbon.

> I remain,
> > Your solitary
> > > Ver solitaire.

Head Quarters Royal Flying Corps,
11.4.17.
Royne blanche comme un lys,

As you have perhaps perceived from a glance at the newspapers a large battle is proceeding. The day before yesterday I went up on a hill to look at it but all one saw was a few of our batteries firing. The Boches had moved back and only on the extreme horizon could one see some of their shells bursting. The Flying Corps have been doing quite magnificently flying in the most atrocious weather low and in snowstorms.

Yesterday I had luncheon with one of the Squadrons and while I was there a machine arrived through a blinding snowstorm and landed.

> I remain
> > Your blainful
> > > Marc Antoine de Muret.

If you get married I will give you a wedding present.

Chose a sensible husband who likes cigars and a decent dinner then you are sure to be happy.

If on the other hand you chose a husband who doesnt care what he eats but bothers about the colour of the carpet you will be unhappy.

Head Quarters R F C B E F France.

14. 4. 17.

What shall be my last day? What shall be yours? Strive not, Leuconoe, to pry into the forbidden future and leave outlandish astrology alone.

It is better to consent to whatever may be; whether Jupiter has many years in store for us still, or whether this winter which is now hurling the Tuscan sea against the rocky shores, shall be the last of all our winters. Be wise; uncork your very best wine; confine your vast hopes in a little room; even as we speak we can hear the beating of time's envious wings.

Enjoy today to the full; do not think about tomorrow.

Yours very truly

Spottiswoode & Co.

Ps the Bowden wire on the Constantinesco Gear is too stiff.

Head Quarters Royal Flying Corps, B.E.F.

15.4.17.

Linda zagaleja,

the man who leads a stainless and innocent life needs neither javelin nor bow and quiver of poisoned arrows, whether he is crossing the moving sands of Africa or climbing the topless rocks of the Caucasus, or wandering in the continent watered by Hydaspes old in story.

Not long ago whilst wandering in the forest of Hesdin at my own vague will, I was making a poem to Juliet and a wolf fled from me, although I threatened him not.

It was a beast such as the savage forests of Germany do not breed, nor the burning desert of Juba, fostress of lions.

Waft me from Indus to the pole; submerge me in the dominion of perpetual mist and rain; place me in the burning heart of the tropics, I shall always love Juliet: the ripple of her speech and her delicious smile.

Yours with kind regards,
H.J. Ryman Ltd.

Head Quarters Royal Flying Corps B.E.F. France.
　20. 4.17.
Princesse d'Elide,

I received the shortest of letters from you last night or more accurately speaking this morning I have been out all day. It has been a spring day at last. Shy clouds in the sky and the buds beginning to open and there is a blackbirds nest in the garden.

Now the time of snow and hail sent by the father of the Gods is over. It has lasted long enough. The thunders of Jove have struck the sacred buildings and made the capital of our dominions quake. The nations have trembled with fear; they believed the years of disaster which terrified Pyrrha were about to return, when Proteus drove his flocks on the high mountains and the fishes were caught in the treetops, in the elm tress where the doves used to moan, and the frighted does swam in the flooded plains.

We saw the yellow Tiber rolling backwards from the Tuscan sea and overflow its left bank to drown the the monuments of Pompilius and the temple of Vesta and to avenge, unsanctioned by heaven, the tears of a wife who was loved too well.

Our youth thinned by the sins of their fathers shall hear of our battles; the sword by which the Hun had better have perished. What god shall we call to our help now that our country is in jeopardy?

With what prayer shall the holy maidens call and call again upon Vesta who turns a deaf ear to them?

Whom shall Jove appoint to atone for our guilt? Come, prophetic sungod, veil thy splendour in a cloud, or if thou wilt, come thou, smiling Goddess of Mount Eryx, with laughter and love fluttering around you, or thou rather, to whom the cries, the clash of arms and the set frown of the murderous fighting man are dear. Alas! art thou not sated with the cruel sport? Has it not lasted all too long? Wilt thou not look upon thy people whom thou hast forsaken, thou, their father?

Or shall it be thou, winged son of lovely Maia, who in the guise of a young hero shalt be called on earth the avenger of Caesar? Hasten not to seek the skies again; stay a long time amongst us, thy people, let not the sight of our crimes speed thee away.

Rejoice here in thy glorious triumphs. Hear with delight yourself acclaimed as father, as Lord of our country, and let not the Huns go on their raids unpunished, in the land of which thou art King.

> Your &
> General Insurance Co Ltd.

Head Quarters Royal Flying Corps, B.E.F. France.
22 4 17.
Rayon d'allegresse,
I think it is really going to be fine today.

A sad thing has happened. Shapashals cigarettes have come to an and and once more in spite of repeated warnings the foolish Freiburg dares to send me a substitute of his own invention: I send it back with scorn hinting at the withdrawal of my custom. It is the third time it has happened.

Wretched are the maidens who dare not love nor drink good wine and who tremble at the sharpness of an uncles tongue.

The winged child of Venus snatches away thy work-basket, thy web, and the service thou givest to industrious Minerva as soon as shining Hilary bathes his well-oiled shoulders in the Thames.

He rides a winged horse better than Bellerophon. He has never been beaten in a race or in a fight.

Unerring too is his aim when the stags in fearful herds skim the plain and he seizes the right moment to confront the wild boar that lurks in the thickets of Hyde Park.

> Your inquisitive,
> Phtos.

Head Quarters Royal Flying Corps, B.E.F. France. 23 4 17.

Chere Madame de Grignan,
I received a short letter from you this morning. It was better than no letter at all. There is still a cold shiver in the air but the sun shines and the bushes are showing little green leaves and the garden is full of oxlips.

I went to look at the Boche machine that was so properly punished for circling over our garden this morning. The captured prisoner said he thought our house was Buckingham Palace. That he was told was no excuse. When I say the captured pilot there were three of them two engines a foot warmer a telescope a periscope a pack of patience cards a concertina a small printing press for printing Menus a cocktail shaker, a bijou typewriter and a green parrot which says Hoch and Gott strafe England if you scratch its head. They set fire to their machine on landing or rather on being forced to land and as the machine was full of bombs
they being of the dangerous sort
exploded with a loud report
and the machine was partially burnt but only partially a lot of it survived.

Ball has brought down another machine today since I wrote to you this morning.

I told you I saw Ned Grosvenor in the Squadron we flew to yesterday. He has got thinner. This comes of not drinking tea at five oclock.

I have learnt to smoke again but I only like gaspers. I can no longer abide Egyptian cigarettes not even if they are rolled by Cleopatra in her salad days.

This comes of giving up things for a time. Give up for a time and you may unwittingly be giving up for ever.

You are quite right in saying that men do not like being bullied. Whether you are right in saying that it is good for them I know not. Some people say that is good for us all to drink Gregorys powder once a week.

There is a blackbird in the garden who is learning to sing quite nicely but he cant, poor thing, learn to *fly*, he has no talent for aviation and always sideslips do what one may.

However it has been settled that he shall be a recording blackbird and live in a nest.

I feel I must go out into the garden partly because Maud*
is there and partly because the office is stuffy.
Your ossified
Charles de Sevigné.

* cf. Tennyson.

Head Quarters R F C B E F France.
April 34 1917.
Oh Posthumus the fleeting years Alas!
The years, Dear Posthumus they pass, they pass. . . .
        Not all thy virtues will prevent
        Old Age, nor bid cold Death relent.
No. Not if with three hundred bulls a day
You try to baulk grim Pluto of his prey,
        Who holdeth fast in durance tame
        Geryon of the triple frame,
And Tityos by the melancholy floss,
Which all who feed on fruitful earth must cross,
        Though mighty monarchs they should be
        Or painful sons of husbandry.
In vain we shun the cruel wounds of war,
Escape the Adriatic's surge and roar,
        And from the hot Sirocco hide,
        That threatens us at Autumntide.
We must behold thy dark flood creep apace,
Cocytus, and the shameful Danaan race,
        And Sisyphus condemned to ply
        A hopeless task eternally.
Yes : we must bid farewell to the kind earth,
To wife and home. the land which gave us birth ;
        Of all thy trees none follow thee
        Except the hated cypress-tree.
A worthier heir shall drain to the last lees
Those casks now guarded by a hundred keys,
        And drench the floor with wine more rare
        Than priests for festal days prepare.
    I remain . Dear Posthumus,
Yours most sincerely,
Flaccus.

Head Quarters Royal Flying Corps, B.E.F. France.
    24.4.17
Sublime decus formosa Laverna,
    Tomorrow is my birthday.
    This morning M Aladin late of the Russian Duma and
M Barzani an Italian called in company with Major Neville
Lytton ci devant artist.
    Then we out in a carriage and not in an aeroplane a Rolls
Royce motor car and we had luncheon with Jack Scott. We
saw Bishop who is another Ball.
    In three days we brought down 76 Huns this is not count-
ing 31 which were claimed as having been driven down out
of control. The weather has been very cold today and cloudy
but it cleared up towards six and is now fine once more. May
it so continue and we shall knock the Boche to pieces. He
is already refusing to fight in the air.
    I have no other news for you.
                                    Yours ardently,
                                        Harpagon.

Head Quarters R F C B E F FRance.
    25.4.17.
Cerise de printemps,
        I went a very long distance in the air today and it was
very cold especially coming back against the wind.
    Yesterday I spent the whole day almost in the air that
is to say in the morning I flew to Belgium and back and
in the afternoon to the South like the swallow.
    Yesterday it was beautiful in the air.
    The sea mysteriously fringed the coloured world and the
lights and shadows made a wonderful chequer board.
    Today it was hideous. The sky was grey and full of rolling
clouds the earth was as colourless as a photograph.
    The fields are scarred and chewed up by the shell fire and
the devastation on the ground beyond the Somme is past belief.
Every single tree has been methodically cut down ; every rose
tree and every Virginia creeper.
    The damage done to the roads has already been repaired
so that this devastation was from a military point of view

waste of time and wasted of labour.   On the way out, we suddenly heard two shots in the grey cloudy space !   Oh ! My !

On the way back we saw a Boche balloon brought down a part of it fell into the Somme at that moment a Nieuport was hovering over us and guns from the ground were firing. My pilot attracted my attention and pointed to the ground. I thought he meant that he was going to land and that the Nieuport was an UN.   However my panic was only momentary.   But Lord how helpless one feels in the isolation of the immense sky.

I used to be the disciple of a foolish philosophy and whilst I was its dupe my prayers to the gods were feeble and tepid.

Today I am compelled to retrace my steps and to seek the road which I had forsaken.

For Jove who more often makes himself felt with cloud and whirlwind has dropped a bolt from the serene blue.   The solid earth, the the rivers which water it, the Styx, the shores of horrid Tenarus and the mountain tops of Atlas, all the universe have felt the shock.

I remain your meretricious,

Mercator.

Head Quarters R.F.C. B.E.F. France

29. 4. 17.

Madame et chère marraine,

I am weary of machines even of undercarriages and interrupter-gears and Aldis sights and centre-sections.

I am weary of machines that fly.

I am still more weary of machines that won't fly and even still more weary of machines that can't fly.

Above all things I am weary, overweary weary to death of motorcars.

I am weary of the war and especially of the war in the air.

I am weary of the constant wonder as to whether those who have flown away will come back.

No words can express my weariness.

YOUR

Lassus viarum militiaeque.

Head Quarters R.F.C. B.E.F. France.
    30.4.17.
Linda di Chamouni,

    I have just come home from flying. Was it in view of the lovely weather agreeable? Not very because of the heat bumps.

    The machine also flew slightly left wing down and the pilot said we barely cleared the trees when leaving the aerodrome at the place from whence we started.

    Coming back was nice for the passenger myself less nice for the pilot who had a sore hand.

    As for me my intense weariness of spirit has not departed.

    Would that I had the wings of a dove or a Sopwith Triplane and could fly far away to the end of the day where the cool and the palm trees are.

                                    Yrs. Jules Sandeau.

            Head Quarters Royal Flying Corps,
                B.E.F. FRANCE.
Dear Animated Bust,

    I have got a very sore throat also a headache also a cold also slight toothache. I feel miserable and out of doors it is radiant and warm and the birds are singing and the crows have built their nests and laid eggs inside them.

    But I am miserable and feel like Death.

    I see in the times that Nan is going to be married shortly at least I suppose it is Nan. How exciting isnt it and what a good thing. He is very nice indeed. I dont know him very well but Bron liked and admired him immensely.

    You had better follow her example and marry at once and without further discussion. Have you chosen a husband? Selfridges is the place.

    Today the communication pilot was ill so we couldnt fly. Instead we went in a motor car. The roads were very dusty. What a lot of interesting things I could tell you were I not so discreet but alas I am discreet.

            As discreet as an owl.
                I am your affectionate
                    Aziola.

Head Quarters Royal Flying Corps,
3. 5. 17.

Perle d'Angleterre,

The surface of the earth is changing its colour. I am reading the Iliad of Homer. It is like a first hand account of the present war : in many respects.

What about my seal? It has not arrived but my birthday has come and gone. I dont know how old I am. Too old to count, the hairs on the side of my head (I have three dozen left) are white now and no longer grey. I am frequently taken for Father Christmas.

Neither the treasures of the rich nor the sceptres and emblems of authority can disperse the troubles of the soul nor the cares which hover round the ceilings of the great.

A man lives happily on little whose only heirloom is an unpretentious saltseller. Fear and greed disturb not his slumbers. Why in so brief a span do we seek after many inventions?

Content with today fret not your soul with the thought of the morrow ; meet your troubles with a laugh, for in this world there is no such thing as complete felicity.

Brief was the fate of great Achilles, whereas Tithonus rotted in a slow decay. Time perhaps will bring to me what time denies to you.

I have but a few acres and a spark of the glory that was Greece ; this is my portion and with it a contempt for what is common and mean.

Your patient,
Job.

A man in the RFC here called Beverly who was carpenter to H Q. blew up his hands with a bomb.

He has blown off three fingers and a thumb from one hand and his thumb from the other hand. This is a great tragedy as he was an excellent carpenter and quite young and it is his only way of earning a living. He may possibly go to your hospital.

If so I want to find out whether at Roehampton they could make him artificial fingers which would be of any use. If he is at your hospital by any chance do get anything done which can be done. M.B.

Head Quarters Royal Flying Corps,
7. 5. 17.
Belle Dame sans culottes,

unspeakably weary as I am I must write to you to say this is the third or fourth day running I have not heard from you. Have you got German measles or English cooking or French leave or Danish butter or perhaps Swedish exercises?

I am quite alarmed but I suppose it is really only a case of your cruel callous cold heart and your frivolous and forgetful spirit. In any case please make good right away. And be the goods once more.

Vex thyself not overmuch=O Maurice=with memories of cruel Juliet; sing no more plaintive elegies because a younger man outshines you in her faithless eyes.

Lycoris is in love with Cyrus, Cyrus adores Pholoe who detests him. But does shall mate with wolves sooner than Pholoe take a lover whom she despises.

I myself when attracted by Mrs. Alfred Lyttelton was kept back in bondage by Ellen the housemaid who was wilder than the waves of the Adriatic that surge in the gulfs of Calabria.

Your loving,
Pliny the middle aged.

Head Quarters R F C B.E.F. France.
9. 5. 17.
Jeune ange aux doux regards,

so it was merely that you were engaged in frivolous pursuits. That was the reason of your silence and your neglect. I am ashamed of you. I am afraid that your heart is like war bread made of sawdust. I have no news to tell you. The blossom is beginning. The lilies of the valley are uncrumpling their leaves. And the war goes on and on on land on sea and in the air and under the earth.

In spite of the fact that there is not one human being in the whole world who is not longing for it to stop.

Write me a page of gossip. Are you wearing the tonneau skirt or the spinning nosedive skirt ?

Yours resignedly,
Herbert Spencer. (Erb)

Head Quarters Royal Flying Corps,
    B.E.F. France.
        12. 5. 17.
Jeune amour plein de mystere,

    I have been out all day with Major Orpen formerly a painter now a Major. It is just time for dinner so I cannot go on writing at present. The post has not come so I dont know whether I have received a letter from you today or not.

    The weather has been hot and dusty with far off hints and rumours of thunder.

    Little did a stupendous dive in a Sopwith Triplane.

    I remain Madam,
        Your sans facaon,
        XXXXXXX Faisnade.
    No. Faisandé.

    Head Quarters R F C
    B E F France.
    16.5.17.
Belle âme qui m'est chère,

    I have just come back from a long and arduous expedition which consisted in receiving and entertaining a bevy or phalanx of Italian Officers and one Lieutenant General and in showing them stores Depots and Squadrons.

    I got up early quite unnecessarily as they were three nearly four hours late.

    A fine exhibition of flying was then given for them in the afternoon.

    They were shown splitpins turnbuckles and paper felt washers for induction pipes.

    In these things they took an intelligent interest at least some of them did. Some of them didnt.

    But in their luncheon they all took an interest.

    I am glad Nan is looking well. Please give her my kind regards if you see her. I have just received three detective stories I find these together with the Iliad of Homer a stirring tale of brave times a solace during these days of stress.

        Yours guestweary,
        Dante Alighieri Rossetti.

Head Quarters R F C
B E F France.
19.5.17.

Riant mensonge,

yesterday I did not write to you. Because I was away in the country in the armies in the Squadrons. I saw Lord Derby. I saw Lord Esher. I saw the C in C. I had luncheon with General Allenby who showed temper with his A D C over the port decanter. I saw Lord Dalmeny and Colonel Grant. I saw Sir Philip Sassoon and General Malcolm and General Higgins.

I saw Major Scott Major Maclean and a Captain German. He is in spite of all temptations an Englishman. A Bosh was frightened down in our lines this morning in his pocket was a theatre ticket admitting him to a private box in the Theatre Royal Cambrai. This he was on the point of destroying when the Intelligence Officer with an eagle eye noticed this and snatched it from him and had it translated into English.

I have no cigarettes that I can smoke. That is to say smoke with pleasure. I have Three Castle cigarettes and I do not like them. And there are no more Shapshal cigarettes to be had for love or money.

I am yours Unserviceable
Raf. 12.

Head Quarters
Royal Flying Corps,
B.E.F. France.
20.5.17.

Songe frivole,

everybody is in a state of trepidation about Russia owing to the panic felt on the subject by our politicians. I do not share this panic. I thing the resignations of Gouchkov and Milioukov were bound to happen and will be fraught with no fatal consequences. Milioukov represented casuistry and compromise and the quintessence of the Girondin spirit. Gouchkov was too Whig. Of course if the Generals all resigned things would be different but I dont believe they will. I feel certain there isnt a chance of Russia making peace. I may be quite

I am no doubt an incorrigible optimist and you will say that the wish fathers my cheerful thought. Not entirely. Experience leads me to be sure that our politicians know nothing about Russia and instinct leads me to believe in Russian stubbornness and resistance.

Russians do things in their own way and their way is quite different from ours.

Their radicals are not like our radicals and in Russia mushrooms agree with the stomach where as in England they disagree with it.

We are awaiting the arrival of Colonel Grant who has not yet come. I am suffering from a dearth of summer socks not too thick. Please order me some at Turnbull and Assers Jermyn Street. They have my size. Or should have. If they havent tell them my foot is the same size as that of the Achilles statue in Hyde Park.

Have you read Wells book about the Finite God? He believes in three Gods but not in one person. One is veiled one is a kind of ferret and the other is an immortal friend who is doing his best in a hopeless situation like Prometheus Bound. It is a schoolboyish book. Halfbaked and cela 'ne tient pas debout. But it his expression of a religious experience : mixed with his ancient rebellion against Exeter Hall which is the only form of Christianity he has come across and which overshadowed his childhood or boyhood or both.

The book will probably annoy the NoGoddites. It will make Catholics smile. Wells knows no history save that of the cheaper books of reference and the Encyclopaedia Britannica.

Yours hopeful
The Man who was.

Very Important.

Evan the other day asked me for a Latin motto for the tanks. I suggested Nihil Obstat which means Nothing stands in the way of par extension there is no objection.

But the question is could it mean nothing stands in the way

129

of physically. I am not at all sure. Please ask Eddy lest the Tanks receive a motto in bad Latin or rather in good Latin misapplied.

Because Evan is delighted but then he doesnt know Latin. Please do this without fail and let me know the result.

YRS
Gra

Head Quarters
   Royal Flying Corps,
    B.E.F. France.
     25.5.17.

Eclatant souvenir,

We are home back returned once more in our nest. I am more dead than alive and what the G must feel like I cant tell. As he had to do the talking the whole time. He is a wonderful man. The head of the French Flying Corps visited us yesterday and before landing did a spinning nose-dive just to show all was well.

I cant yet make out the Greek: Greek in English characters is very difficult to read. I cant tell you how good the cigarettes taste nor can I tell you how beautiful the seal is.

I am glad the tank motto is all right. Evan wrote and said he was delighted with it. He added I have got the credit for it at present. You will get the credit later.

What does that mean? I could understand if he said I get the credit and you will never get it. Or if he said You get the credit for it of course. But his strange compromise beats me. It is however I expect thoroughly characteristic of the Charteris breed.

Hillary arrives tomorrow. Very cleverly he got into direct communication with the G. who sent a car to Paris to fetch him! I should never have dared suggest such a thing and had he applied to me I should have tremblingly said there was nothing to be done. The moral of this is always apply to the fountain head in all things and you will get what you want. Never consult underlings.

Yesterday and the day before we visited 9 Squadrons and three Kite Balloons.

And the G. spoke to all the pilots and saw everything. He rides the whirlwind and directs the storm and kindles in every one he sees an undying spark.

But he was white with fatigue afterwards. I cant tell you how tiring it must be for him since I myself who only look on am worn to a shred.

Ave atque Aurevoir,
Miser Catullus.

Head Quarters
Royal Flying Corps,
B.E.F. France.
26.5.17.

Lampe joyeuse,

the socks are perfect both as to texture shade colour and weight. The ties are exquisite and match the colour of the war landscape without attracting the attention of hostile aircraft. So they want an English motto for Tanks. Diable. English is an analytic and not a synthetic language. Have they thought of that? Have they realised that what you can say in one word in Latin takes twelve words to say in English.

I can think of nothing except Die Hard or Last Ditch. Or Thorough or la fumee passe le tank reste. Which God knows is true. Hillary arrives this afternoon from Paris. I want you to impress upon him that it was a wonderful thing and an act of great friendliness on the part of the G. to send a car to Paris to meet and fetch him and to have him here to stay : vu many things : one that he is very busy, very tired very much harassed and obliged to cope with a stream of unbidden guests including Joynson Hicks M.P.

The weather is gorgeous. It is like it used to be before the war when men and women went to Ascot and sat out in gardens in the middle of the night while others danced in ball rooms. Do you remember those days?

I am republishing Brons Poem in a small pamphlet. . Blackwell at Oxford is doing it. It should be out by the time you get this letter. You will be able to get it at shops. It is a great comfort to me that people liked it and people of different kinds and want to have a copy of it.

I have had two cheerful letters from the Russian Army both from officers. Both say that perfect order reigns in their ranks.

Let us hope this is so.

Je vous salue,

Yours always

Paul de Musset.

Head Quarters R F C.
B.E.F. France.
28.5.17.

Chere Carmoisine,

H. left this morning. I hope he enjoyed himself. He was in a very nice mood. I think he is very tired and there seems to be no remedy for that but to stop work which he cant do.

We are all very tired and the Huns are more tired still. Their fatigue is increased by having nothing to eat at all but a few sawdust dolls.

Yours in the earnest hope of hearing from you presently

Yrs faithfully

Gustavus.

Head Quarters R F C B E F France.
29.5.17.

Parole dorée,

it is a dud day. Clouds about a thousand some rain.

I have been made a chevalier of the legion of honour ! ! ! ! ! ! Wonders will never cease. And nothing is too extraordinary not to happen.

Hillary has a new stunt of "ritual" breaking . . . He imagines something is a ritual so he sets out to break it . . .

For instance he thinks it is a ritual to have tea for break-fast . H the second morning he was staying here asked for beer for breakfast. He knew there was no beer in the house because he was informed of this as soon as he entered the house so he simply said it to show off to break the ritual. Nobody cared. I wasnt there or he wouldnt have done it. We had luncheon with some shy and silent sailors who were busy eating their luncheon. Hillary said their silence was some kind of ritual in reality it was their innate lack of vivacity. He passes the port round the wrong way after dinner on purpose. This is also to break the ritual but this is a superstition. Yrs Charles le Timide.

June 1.1917.
Head Quarters Royal Flying Corps,
B.E.F. France.
Esclave couronee,
It is as you see the first of June. You did ili not to write to me for two days. The time you chose not to write to me coincided with the Whitsuntide holidays so I got no letters at all during that festal period. I have been out all the afternoon but all the people I wanted to see and to whom I paid visits were out so I left cards and went away.

On the way back I gave an officer who was going on leave a lift. He had been seven times over the top. He had not been on leave for eighteen months. He belonged to the New Army.

That is I think all the news I have to tell you. No, there is more. Captain Seagrave has gone to England because his leg where he was badly wounded in the air hurts him so he no longer works in this office. Should you see him be kind to him and say to him
            Dear Captain Seagrave
            Do try to be brave.
                    Yrs Constant Benjamain.

Head Quarters Royal Flying Corps,
        B.E.F. France.
    2.6.17.
O Kalee,
        today one of the finest things happened which have happened during the war.
    A certain Corps complained of some machines flying low

over its lines. So a star pilot called Bishop was given a free
hand to deal with the matter as he thought best.

He went to a Hun aerodrome and there he saw the Hun
machines all spread out and ready starting their engines.

This was very early in the morning.

He flew right down low as if he was going to land.

He shot one mechanic who was starting an engine dead
and disposed of that machine. Another which just got off
he drove into a tree where it crashed a third he brought down
a few hundred yards from the aerodrome. Then he came home.
He went down to about twenty feet. Think of the audace of it.

Mr. Joynson Hicks and Sir Charles not Sir Arthur
Nicolson arrived last night and are touring round. They dine
with us tonight. The day has been hot and sultry.

yr feverish Blaise Pascal.

Head Quarters Royal Flying Corps,
       B.E.F. France.
           5.6.17.

Very hot it has been today, Belle Bourbonnaise, I have
been to six Squadrons. I had luncheon with one and tea with
another.

Last night there was an Old Etonian dinner at the Lord
Roberts Memorial Hall.

There were three hundred Old Etonians present. I knew
about 5 by sight. All my contemporaries were Lieutenant
Generals. They sang accompanied by the Coldstream Band
and after dinner eveything in the room was broken all the
plates all the glass all the tables the chandeliers the windows
the doors the people.

A bomb raid was nothing to it.

Lord Cavan presided and made a very good speech in Latin.
It was answered by someone else a scholar in bad Latin. The
guests spoke English.

There was not one representative of the Julian and Billy
generation. They have been all killed.

The rest were either much older older than me.

Or much younger than the war.

Yours Old Etonian.

Head Quarters R F C B E F France.
6.6.17.
Poularde fine,
the post goes at an inconvenient time so it may befall that one day you will get no letters from me and on the next two.

I hope you will be successful in the matter of the ice machine. I think you will, difficult as the commission is. I trust in your genius as well as in your talent assisted by your personal charm and not hindered by the beauty of your countenance.

It is thundering and raining cats but not dogs.
Yours distracted,
Chevalier de Boufflers.

Head Quarters Royal Flying Corps, B E F France.
7.6.17.
Chatoyante emeraude,
I hope you will manage to get an ice machine.

It is not for myself as you will have understood. It is for a friend who needs it as he lives on a parching aerodrome under the dogstar.

Mr. Joynson Hicks went away yesterday.

He said there was not a workman in England who didnt know him by sight.

J'aime Dijon et la beaute
De ses vignes fleuries,
I am yours without sealing wax,
l'aimable Bacchus.

Head Quarters R.F.C.B.E.F. France.
June 7. QOQU.
Ma Fanchon,
The weather today has been clear.
Mr Joynson Hicks is very conceited.
Your most true
Blue.

Head Quarters Royal Flying Corps,
　　　B.E. F. France.
　　9.6.17.
Bonjour belle que voila,
　　　as further news comes in about the victory the larger
and the richer the event appears and proves to be. It is the
finest day in the air we have ever had. We entirely prevented
the Boche Flying Corps from working and our artillery work
in cooperation with aircraft went without a hitch. But what
is that to you?
　　Let us rather discuss more insignificant things the colour
of Chloes hair or the size of Daphne's hat.
　　It is hot. The summer is arriving in great strides bearing
in one hand a poppy and in the other a basket full of straw-
berries.
　　My brother Hugo looked in last night after dinner. With
him came Lord Osmond Beauclerc.
　　　　As for me I am still
　　　　　　your ruminating,
　　　　　　　　　Pauv' gas.

　　Head Quarters Royal Flying Corps,
　　　B.E.F. France.
　　　4.7.17.
Enfant de Cypris,
　　　A Russian pilot came here called Nolken. He had a
happy day at the Depot. He was very nice.
　　I have been made a Major. I am sorry to part with the
title of Captain. A Captain as you know combines the fire of
the subaltern with the discretion of the field officer. I say
Goodbye to the fire of the subaltern.
　　I am sorry Beerbohm Tree is dead.
　　I have read Bourgets latest book. It is a good story spun
out with rather tiresome comments. His books would be
excellent if they were written by someone else.
　　Ne forcons point notre talent.
　　　　I remain your affectionate,
　　　　　　Major
　　　　Baring.

Head Quarters R F C
B E F France.
22.7.17.
Adorable sujette,
a violent thunderstorm is happening.
I am reading a pretty book called la Bête Humaine by
Zola. It is all about the puff-puff but it is not in spite of this
suitable reading for the nursery.
The Russian reverse is in a way fortunate it may give
them a Government and discipline. Out of the chaos I hope
a new order may arise.
Let us be cheerful.
For however badly we may feel the Boches are feeling
worse.
And I remain,
Yours ever Maitre Jaques.

Head Quarters Royal Flying Corps, B.E.F. France.
24.7.17.
Gentil rossigolet,
thank you for your letter of yesterday. Yesterday we
visited two French Squadrons. The day before yesterday the
Commander In Chief of the American Army and his Staff
visited us. They were shown the aeroplane repair section the
Balloon stores the stores and three Squadrons.
Sloly, the pilot, flew to them and did a spin down to
within 40 feet of the ground. I felt sick. It was an accident
he was calculating *glasomer* and not by the instruments.
But all is well that lands well. The day before yesterday Ian
Hendersons propeller came off in the air jammed the con-
trols and he had to plunge into the earth having no control over
his machine. It was broken into little bits he himself received
no scratch.
I liked General Pershing very much. His Staff as we drove
through a cloud of dust said : "I think I know the taste of
this landscape now."
In the meantime I send you my best love,
Your
Fredon babillard frétillard.

Head Quarters R.F.C. B.E.F. France.
31.July.

Eclat foudroyant des lumieres celestes,

It has been a thoroughly misty day cloudy that is to say no sun and some rain, in spite of this the flying machines of the R F C flew down low through the clouds on to the Boche aerodromes and roads and shot at people driving in harmless motor cars and killed them. They also shot German machines on German aerodromes. In fact they thoroughly enjoyed themselves but if you could see the weather you would indeed wonder. One pilot who is called the War Baby and who claims to be seventeen but looks more like twelve shot a fat German dead in his motor

The German had previously threatened him with a pistol but in vain.

Yrs Isaac Pitman.

Head Quarters R.F.C.B.E.F. France.
9.8.17.

Ardente croix du sud,

Thank you for the letter which I received last night and which amused me.

Yesterday we went into the battle area. To Messines.

The moment you walk into the battle zone the first thing that strikes you or rather me is the instant and sudden silence broken only by the noise of shells.

We walked to Messines. As we walked the Boches were shelling some batteries to the right of us and some batteries behind us and the shells whistled over our heads like little trains. As or when we reached Messines itself the shells were falling on it so we made a strategic movement to the left.

All the ground is pitted with huge holes but it is all overgrown with tangled weeds and wild vegetation of every kind mangel wurzel and hemp and grass and concertina wire and every now and then a dead Boches boots and bones.

We wandered through devious ways to Wytshaete, itself now a heap of rubbish and up a hill where a lot of bricks are which were once a church. There we sat and watched big shells falling into Ostaverne wood in front of us.

Our batteries retaliating noisily also.

All this was the quiet daily hate of an off day as no fighting proper is going on there.

Then the shells. . . it was a grey day and no observation being possible the Boche was just doing a round of registered targets. . . . veered in our direction and and we retired in time to retire with dignity and not to have to retire in an undignified fashion, and only just in time as we watched from the other side of the road the shells falling on the place where we had just been sitting.

The we had luncheon at the roadside and after inspecting one of the vast mine craters we returned once more to the land of the living.

Yrs egregious
Exsul.

Head Quarters
Royal Flying Corps,
B.E.F. France.
10.8.17.

Invincible charme,

Linky is staying here also the brothers Salmond: Jack anf Geoff on his way to Egypt. Colonel Duval comes here this afternoon. He now commands the French Flying Corps.

I have a bad headache. I have taken aspirin So much for news. You will find the shorthand much easier than it looks. It gets easier and easier as you get on. Let me know when you wish for a letter in shorthand. I am reading South Wind. I find it a little bit fatiguing. It is a peace rather than a war book. My brain is like an addled egg,

> unmothered in a nest forlorn,
Too weak to work, too proud to beg,
My brain is like an addled egg,
I wish I were in Winnipeg,
> Amidst the candy and the corn,
My brain is like an addled egg
> unmothered in a nest forlorn.

Your loving
Maikäfer.

Head Quarters R F C
   B E F France.
      11.8.17.
Tour D'Argent,
      the weather is uncertain. You are right in thinking
the country a noisy place it is. There is a bird here which
begins singing at dawn. It sings three notes wide apart and
at a sharp angle over and over again. The other birds follow
its example. So far so good. You say how charming but
very soon motor bicycles join the concert and aeroplanes and
lighting sets and then the noise becomes irksome. I know
someone here who has been to Vaynol and knows it well.
Yesterday a French Colonel came here and pinned the cross
of the Legion of Honour on to my breast. It has two long
and very sharp pins. He dug them them in to my too too
solid flesh. I bore the pain for one second but as I noticed
that he was pressing the pins deeper and deeper into my breast
I finally uttered a shrill squeak Then he let go.
                                                Yrs
                                          Post Meridian.

      August the nineteen nineteen hundred and seventeen
         Head Quarters
            Royal Flying Corps,
               B.E.F. France.
Volage bergère,
      (I mean shepherdess not armchair) I heard from you
last night but I cannot congratulate you on the length of your
letters
      It is fine and has been very fine all day but the strong west
wind is disastrous to our air tactics. and favourable to the
Boche machines who can fly home with ease and celerity. I
am reading a book written by a schoolboy about school called
the Loom of life no the Loom of youth.
      It is remarkable that he should have been able to write
it. Its main intention I think is to make parents' flesh
creep .
                  Your most sincere acquaintance,
                     Honeycomb radiator.

Head Quarters Royal Flying Corps, B.E.F. France.
23.8.17.
Majesté si pompeuse et si fière,
    it is raining after a very sultry and hot day which was
yesterday and a stifling night. After dinner a Boche machine
came over and bombed. The archies banged at it. The
searchlights flitted round it the summer lightning flickered in
the distance. We did not know till this morning that any
bombs had been dropped. And I dont yet know where they
fell. This morning I broke the window inadvertently of our
motor car a Rolls Royce. The window was half up and I
shut the door too emphatically. I did not bang the door, but
the window vacillated and finally collapsed into a thousand
smithereens and now we must needs get a new window and
this in war time is as you know very difficult.
    I did not hear from you yesterday. I suspect that you
write more seldom than you used to to do. How unlike your
obedient Servant,
        Le vieux Captif.

Head Quarters Royal Flying Corps,
    25.8.17.
Feuille éphémère,
    No post last night on account of the roughness of the
sea. Had there been a post would there have been a letter
from you? That is the question. Commandant Du Peuty
stayed with us last night and told us some interesting things
about the battle of Verdun where he had been. The quality
of the prisoners taken he said was bad. One division on being
asked why they had taken no prisoners said Nous n' avons pas
l'habitude d'en prendre.
    The weather is uncertain and cool.
    I have not heard from Hillary for many a long day. I
wonder where he is.
    I must now stop as I have to write on business to the Earl
of Athlone.
    Have you heard of the Earl of Athlone?
            Yrs most constant,
                Mono Soupape.

Head Quarters R F C B E F France.
27.8.17.
Festina Lente,
the other morning I think I forgot to tell you that I went down into the town in company with Major Sir Philip Sassoon Bart, we passed in a street a maiden with bright red hair and Philip wishing to pay her a compliment said to her vous avez de tres jolies cheveux Mademoiselle. But the effect of the compliment was spoilt for as he said it he tripped up over his silver spurs and fell on his face on the pavement

The weather is atrocious. I seldom hear from you these days. The post is as barren as a wilderness.

Yours truly,
G A K LUhani.

Head Quarters Royal Flying Corps, B.E.F. France.
29.8.17.
Seraphim du Soir,
the gale has somewhat abated but the squalls continue to drift in from nowhere. Captain Acton R N arrived here last night a self invited guest. He had a toothache and was peevish at the thoughts of nearly having to sleep in a hut. This was averted however so all was well.

Yesterday we went to present Guillemer with his D S O. He was covered with medals from head to breast French Russian Belgian Servian Montenegrin Italian. But no German nor Austian. He is very nice but looks very ill and white.

I gave him your best love and he said he remembered meeting you years ago in the Bois de Boulogne. I said that no doubt you remembered it too and that at any rate if you did you would certainly take pains not to forget it. Then he looked pensive and said "Est elle toujours aussi belle?" I sighed and said you were more beautiful than ever. Then we both sighed.

Then we had tea. Tomorrow Lord Cowdray arrives.
We shall say to him on arrival
"Hail Thane of Cowdray!"

Yours long suffering,
De la Rue.

142

Head Quarters R F C B E F France.
31.8.17.
oiseau des isles merveilleuses
     Do not think your letters are dull they are not. The smallest detail interests me. I like to know what flowers you plant and what you have for dinner. What the gardener said and what the weather is like and where you drove to in the afternoon. The weather is fouler than words can express.
     Lord Cowdray arrived last night. He is the Head of the Air Board but the only mention of anything connected with the air suffocates him with boredom. He is a kind old man but no longer in his prime. We are a funny nation to do these things in war time. I have mastered all the principles of Pitmans shorthand. All I want now is practice. I have done all the exercises in the book up to No 97.
                       Your peevish,
                       Louis —Xavier de Ricard.

Head Quarters Royal Flying Corps, B.E.F. France.
4.9.17.
Elitre d'azur,
     last night was a fine night after a fine hot day. This is very surprising. We were bombed again last night and again the antiaircraft guns set up a deafening shindy and rained bits of shell on land on sea and the game was repeated three times running robbing us of our rest. A boche machine only came once. This will soon become as dangerous a spot as London.
     You will I am sure send me the soap and I would be much obliged if you would do something else for me. Choose the most luxurious shop you know where one buys knives cigarette cases and dressing cases. A shop like Aspreys or a better one if there is a better one and ask them to send me their catalogue. I want an object but cannot order it without a catalogue.
     Lord Cowdray went away yesterday. On leaving he presented General Trenchard with a small box containing 25 indifferent cigars.
                   I remain yours unrewarded
                   The Passionate Pilgrim.

Head Quarters R.F.C.B.E.F. France.
4.10.17.
Mobile etoile aux ailes de lumiere,
I have been to London and back since I last wrote to
you nor was I able to visit even a shop so busy was I, so tied
to the antechambers of the War Office and the Air Board. If
you were in London you must have felt the results of my
arrival because as I flew over in one machine and T in another
and his shorthand clerk in a third our arrival was reported as
an air raid and the alarm was given.
We had a lovely crossing over the haze of the Channel but
encountered some clouds near Tonbridge and the General went
back to Lym and I went on to Croydon and landed and there
I waited for two mortal hours in sickening anxiety as he did
not turn up and telephoning was impossible owing to the
reported air raid.
In London which I motored up to I could not get any
news either and finally I was obliged to telephone to France
where they told me he had landed at Lym.
It was a very anxious time. As the last I had seen of
him was diving down into the mist and the shorthand clerk
who arrived in another machine said he had seen the remains
of a crashed machine in a ploughed field being given first aid.
I stayed at Johns house the night and dined there. The
next morning after more war office and more air board we
motored to Dover and crossed the Channel in a destroyer.
I hope I may never go through such an experience again.
Todays battle is going exceedingly well.
We also are plentifully bombed here when the nights are
fine. I hate it.
I remain yours Autumnal,
Teo Fani.

Head Quarters Royal Flying Corps, B E F France.
17.10.17.
Belle Fille,
thank you for your letter which I got last night. Yesterday I took Major Orpen to a Squadron where I think he
enjoyed himself and today he will probably paint a portrait of

a pilot namely Rhys Davids who only left Eton a short time
ago and has brought down a whole bevy of Huns.

We are going on quite a long expedition tomorrow or the
day so you will not hear from me for some time.

Please send me news of Conny and any details you have.
Is he in the Admiralty? Nobody has had news of him for
months and his silence has caused universal anxiety

Yrs

Faux Fuyant.

Head Quarters R F C B E F France.

29.10.17

Dearest Ju

I have just seen in the newspaper the news of your
mothers death. One can only be thankful that her long long
sufering is over. But it is difficult to realise that one will
never see her again and that something so brilliant and shining
and unique has been extinguished. That "all that is ended"

Bless you

Yrs mb

H Q R F C B E F France.

12 11 17.

Dearest Ju

I have not written because I have been travelling all
the week. 350 miles there 350 miles back and 90 miles while
there. On the way back I stopped with Chandon but not
with Moet.

I am very exhausted.

I may be coming to England soon for a day or two but not
on leave so I shall probably be tied hand and foot.

It is cold and the war has not stopped and ministries seem
to be falling like packs of cards and populations are peevish
and whole armies are surrendering and Russia is having another
revolution in spite of all this I have seldom felt so optimistic.
It is strange but true.

Yrs M.B.

Head Quarters R F C B E F France.
23.11.17.
Chere Estree Blanche,

I received to day one of the greatest shocks of my life. I was going to say of surprise but strictly speaking it is not surprise because we both anticipated it.

It is to this effect : I received a letter from Hillary in which he says, Harmsworth has come back and is directing affairs again. but not very successfully : but he is determined to help the war within his lights : Only he is vain and insufficient.

The next thing that we shall hear is that he is a sad man. We shall then hear that he will save his soul. Finally we shall hear that he is a good man.

                    Yours en hiver et en ete,

                                        Passapartout.

Head Quarters R.F.C.B.E. F. France.
4.12.17.
O rose blanche et solitaire,

        as you see I have come to an end of my decent and moderate writing paper and I am now compelled to use these huge sheets. It has been very cold today indeed but very fine. I had luncheon with D G T. I dont know what that means but he manages the railways. Winston Churchill arrives tonight to dine and sleep. I am vexed by many things.

I am reading Lord Morleys recollections. They are written with great dignity and elegance. He is full of Kultur. But the doings of politicians cannot fail to disgust two such innocents as yourself and your devoted,

                    '   Almeric. (Not Paget).

Head Quarters Royal Flying Corps, B E F France.
5.12. 17.
Cloche éperdue au vertige du ciel,

        I thought I had written to you today but I find on searching the letter box that I have not. The cold continues to be merciless and my bed room is like a south polar expedition. In fact I cannot sleep whether this be from the cold I know not as my bed feels warm but I wake up and stay awake. Winston and Bendor stayed here last night. Winston looked worried and anxious. He was most amiable to me and answered when he was spoken to which was more than he did the other day when I met him at the C in C s house. Bendor I adore. I adore Bendor. Ned Grosvenor came in after dinner. If Ned is Bendors Uncle and I am Neds Uncle I suppose I am Bendors Great Uncle? In this case what relation. . . . but I will not finish the sentence but leave it to your delicate sense.

Write me all the news and the ondits and the what we want to knows.

I pant for gossip which is divine.

Your etc
Fana la Tulipe.

Head Quarters R.F.C.
B E F France.
6.12.17.

Donna leggiadra,

I had luncheon today with some French Officers. It is always amusing to have luncheon with the French. In the first place the food is excellent and well cooked. In the second place they all talk together gaily. I enjoyed myself. I suppose you are by this time up and about. The weather continues to be severe. The night air is most penetrating and blankets afford one but a slender protection.

Someday or other the war will come to an end. I shall not be sorry.

Have you read the Life of Keats? It is most sad.

I have just been reading the life of Milton. I think that if he had been your husband you would have been very unhappy. You would have had to read him the psalms in hebrew every day and if you had asked what it all meant he would have said never mind.

Your obedient,
Rex Poode.

11.12.17.
Head Quarters R.F.C.
B.E.F.

O Amabel,

so Jerusalem has been taken again after an interval of 733 years but Hillary says the Christians lost it in July and the Times says October. This is the way historians disagree. Please ask him whether he is right or wrong. It was very tactful of General Allenby not to shell it and I expect he will refrain from all theatrical antics in the manner of his enrtry.

So as to contrast with the behaviour of the German Emperor.

The weather is again raw and far from pleasant.

So I will draw to a close and subscribe myself yours faithful
Geoffrey de Bouillon.

Head Quarters . R.F.C.
B.E.F. France.
12.12.17.

Blest single siren,

I have just come in after an extensive tour. Nobody appears to have wooden undercarriages in the RE8 yet which is perplexing. I have a great longing to go to Jerusalem now that it belongs to General Allenby. But I suppose that you would rather go to great Seleucia built by Grecian Kings or where the sons of Eden long before dwelt in Telassar.

Yours with the kindest regards,
Jacques Tournebroche.

Head Quarters R.F.C.
B.E.F. France.
23.12.17.

The Eve of Cristmass Eve.

Silver-buskined Nymph,

Neither did I write to you yesterday as I was out all day but not shopping as you were, far from it. We started at eight and got to the place where the Empress Eugenie used to give her famous little parties at a quarter to twelve. Then after a quarter of an hours conversation we had luncheon. After luncheon a conference which lasted till half past two and then we started home.

We reached a sharp turning when a camion automobile ran in to us but the icy road on which we skidded saved us from the worst and the axle was undamaged and the only damage done was to the mudguard. A little further on we met two lorries at right angles across a steep and slippery hill. We managed to get round them but having done so the wheels of the Rolls Royce refused to turn round and we had to dig in get stones and sand and chains and spades and ropes and pursuade the vehicle to go up hill an arduous and long task. It was in the end successfully accomplished but the result was that we took five hours to get home. At dinner an American Major told me a story which was unfortunately interrupted long before the point had been reached. The cold is beyond all words. When I got back last night I found your very nice Christmas present. I did not get your letter till this morning and I thought at first that the volumes were Mr Bains idea of a pocket Milton. I was annoyed with him but now that I know that it was your idea of a pocket Milton my point of view has entirely changed. It is a very nice Milton and I prefer the covers to leather covers. But your idea of my pockets must be an exaggerated one. My pockets are of the kind that hold one pocket handkerchief one match box a piece of string a pocket book and a jujube but no more. The three volumes cannot be held by the pocket nor even one of them but no matter. It shall not be considered as a pocket Milton but as a table or dessert Milton which is a very nice thing to have and in some ways better than a pocket Milton. The book also contains some interesting notes.

Tomorrow is Christmas Eve. One naturally wonders how many more Christmas Eves we shall have to endure darkened by the shadow of war and overhung by the threats of airraids.

As for me I am finished. My spirit is broken my morale is deplorable my feet are covered with chilblains my fingers are stained with the nicotine of Virginian cigarettes. My hairs which are grey and few in number want cutting, my shoes worn in the evening have got holes in the soles of them, my boots pinch me and are as cold as vaults.

149

Apart from all this I am in very good spirits and I think the war prospects are much better than they were last Sunday. Why? I cannot tell.

I had a nice letter from Hillary two days ago.

I am writing you this long two paged letter because it is Christmas time and I have no Christmas card to send you. I send you instead my best wishes my hopes my prayers, my faith and all my love.

I remain,

Silver-buskined nymph,

Your melancholy Dane,

not Hamlet, but,

Karl Gjellerup.

Head Quarters R F C B E F France.
27 ;12 ;17.

Queen of the stars so gentle so benign,

Christmas is over. We had tepid turkey and cold bread sauce and flat champagne and port made of furniture polish. After dinner there was a concert. The electric lighting was wonderful as it would be managed by mechanics and the best electricians in the world. It was better than Reinhardt or the Moscow Art Theatre or Gordon Craig.

A strong man gave an exhibition of strength.

But the assistants who had ill rehearsed their parts nearly killed him by stamping on the wrong portions of his body when he was trying to lift up a dumbell weighing 200l lbs.

The ground is deep with snow. We intend to come to England for some days in a day or so.

I wish you the compliments of the season and remain

yours unsolaced,

Thomas Clarkson.

[In December 1917 Trenchard returned to England as Chief of the Air Staff. Maurice Baring accompanied him, returning to France in May 1918 when the General was appointed to command the Independent Air Force.]

Head Quarters 8th Brigade.

Royale geniture,

we have arrived and I found a letter from you.

We went to Paris and of course the shops were shut as they always are if one goes to Paris for a day or a few hours. We dined at the Ritz. It was very hot. The next day we started for this place. Two thermos bottles were bought before starting one by me and one by Ravenscroft. But scarcely had we travelled a kilometre before my thermos bottle which was full of coffee first began to leak peevishly but firmly and finally broke and had to be thrown away. It cost 23 francs. We stopped for luncheon at a nice little dark hotel. The G. very impatient by coffee time and rather naughty like a child who wants to get away from its tea. Then we went on and arrived here about six thirty. It is a delicious chateau in a garden in the flower beds there are potatoes instead of flowers and it belongs to an old lady who who is eighty three and who walks about as hale as Queen Victoria used to be when she was alive.

We are supposed to go to Paris again on the 28th.

Please send me a book to read but not more than one.

Yrs etc W. Straker. LTD.

Head Quarters Independent Force or as some wit called it Independent Farce. Such is our new official title superscription and address. PLEASE NOTE.

June 7 1918.

Amulette inconnu,

I have been roving the country like rover. Right across France and back and right across France and back breathlessly.

The weather is perfect. This is a beautiful and dignified old chateau nesting on the top of a small village with a bridge and a river at the bottom of it. There is a garden with trees and pond full of carp.

I dont suppose I shall hear from you for sixteen weeks. The General sends you his love at least he would if he knew I was writing to you.

As for me, I feel like a worn out carcase.

Yours etc,
Carte Taride.

Head Quarters Independent Force. RAF BEF France.
    June 24 1918. Saint Jean Baptiste.
Paisante, that is to say Plaisante,
        the mail has not yet come so I dont know whether I
have heard from you or not but I hope I have. I had a letter
from Philip. H gave much news about you amongst other
things that you had *bought* Louis house. Is this true? I
didnt understand you had done that. I told you about the
man who stole 12 eggs four ducks a fish a fox rug a doily four
new blouses and a petticoat from a house in the village? And
a pair of nail scissors. It was thought Heaven knows why to
be a tramp. Well yesterday the stolen articles with the exception of the nail scissors were all put back in a parcel into the
garden.
        Have you read Remnants by Desmond MacCarthy there
are some very amusing things in it.
        My Poems have been reprinted. They look better but the
publisher has still not done what I wanted : to print each one
on a separate page. I shall make him do it in time.
                                        Yours etc
                                            Tintrin.

Head Quarters Independent Force. RAF. BEF. France.
    25 June 1918.
Belle et blanche,
        thank you very much for yesterdays letter. I always
thought that Louis house was in Sussex. I shall be amused
to hear what Hillary says on the subject. Let me know. Did
you get a letter from the Child ? He wrote to you the other
day. We have luncheon with Castelnau today. It is very
fine. I am cheered by the Italian news.
        Otherwise I have nothing to tell you. The carp which
ate the Generals cigar by mistake is much better.
        It was able to swim to the surface of the pond yesterday.
        Bishop was sent for by the Canadian Government to go
home so before starting he went up into the air and shot down
five Huns. The he took the train fo Canada via London.
                                        Yrs etc
                                    Lambert and Butler.

Head Quarters Independent Force. RAF BEF France.
26.June. 1918.

Dear Ju,

The General got a telephone message last night from Salmond to say Ian Henderson had been killed. He has written to David. I dont like writing before these things are in black and white but by the time you get this letter it will. In any case will you send off these two letters for me as soon as you get them. unless by some unhoped-for chance it turns out not to be true. It breaks my heart.

YrM

Head Quarters Independent Force RAF BEF France.
2. July 1918.

Dear Fatima (Cigaret),

the night before last we went to see the machines start and come back from the night expeditions to Hunland. It is quite uncanny to see the great monsters fly off into the sunset and disappear and then you hear them much later humming in the darkness and circling round like great moths till they land.

Have you read the Mystery of the Downs. It is exceedingly exciting, nor did I guess the murderer till the very end. I recommend it to you to while away your time in your new country seat.

How far by the way is it from London?

I remain
Yours Ever
Luciano Folgare. Futurista.

Head Quarters Independent Force RAF.
BEF.France.
July 10. 1918.

Dear tres chere Juliet,

thank you for the letter I got yesterday and for the letter that I did not get today. It rained slightly yesterday after a prolonged spell of scorchingly hot weather. A tragedy

153

of far reaching import happened the other day in Paris. A great deal of glass had been broken by the German bombs if this were not enough damage done my eyeglass was shattered by the string breaking. I enclose a fragment and I would be infinitely obliged to you if you could see your way to go to an eyeglass shop and choose me three of the same diameter and quality and have them sent to me to the above mentioned place. As it is I see nothing. I am like Wotan blind in one eye. Sir Walter Lawrence has arrived. He is to be here permanently. He is a delightful old man. Do you know him? I have just heard from Hillary, a most amusing letter. He mentions your having bought Otham but makes no comment.

The Child is well. He thrives in the extreme heat but as soon as it gets a little cooler he droops.

His temper is fair.

                    Your obedient
                            Arthur Black.

The publishers reprinted my poems and they look nicer but he did not do what I asked him. Publishers are obstinate and seldom perform what they promise. They say Yes but they mean No.

Head Quarters Independent Force. RAF BEF France.
    13.7.18.
Belle Amelie,

I have not heard from you for days and days and days. I hope you are well. I went to the city of Langres today where the pocketknives are made and where there are a number of Renaissance houses.

Yesterday one of the chinese labourers engage on making aerodromes was delivered of a child. This caused great surprise. It is unprecedented in the annals of labour and war work.

But the chinese always were an original people.

The soap and the salt are very gratifying.

I recommend you to read the Humphries Touch. It is amusing but not as amusing as it might have been.

            I am yours
                Candide.

Head Quarters Independent Force. RAF BF France.
22 July 1918.
Soeur de Philomele,
          the Chinese have struck. This the reason. They were
supplied with American bread. It became impossible to supply
them with American bread any longer so they were given an
equal quantity of French bread which is better. They then
struck because they said the French bread had holes in it. And
therefore they lost on the transaction. That is I think all the
news. Lord Weir arrives here this week and later David. I am
glad David is coming. I think it will do him good. Did you
notice my Sonnet in the Times about Icarus?
          Down with the Boches is our battle cry.
                    your
               Mongibelo.

Head Quarters Independent Force, RAF BEF France.
27. July 1918.
Dear Mrs Kendal,
          thank you very much for your two letters. I have not
written lately owing to being out all day and missing post after
post. The Lord Weir not of Hermiston but of Eastwood not
East Lynne has been staying here and with him Sir Maurice
Bonham Carter late of 10 Downing Street. They were shown
eveything in three hectic days. I only had influenza for half
a day. I cured it by eating a black currant and taking a pinch
of snuff.
          The news is very invigorating. Personally I felt happy
from the moment when in your drawing room after dinner the
night Sommy was there Hillary said it was all up with the
allies. I remember making him repeat that and then looking
at you with a radiant smile of relief. I think the war was won
at Liege in 1914. Beacuse if at the beginning of a game of
bridge you make one mistake one bad mistake you may save
the Slam but you cant make the odd trick.
          The Chinese strike is over. A man came who understood
Chinese and settled the matter in a moment.
          Castelnau dined here the other night and was charming. I
am yours faithful Tuxedo.

Head Quarters Independent Force. RAF.BEF France.
July 30 1918.
Dear Madame Patey,

David arrived here last night. It broke my heart to see him. He was perfectly natural and just himself. I think it will do him good to be here for a little. I cant send you the Poem as I have not got it at least not to give if you know what I mean. It came out in the Times on a Thursday. Geoffrey Dawson wrote and told me he preferred it to the original (which shows lamentable bad taste on his part) and that it had had an immense success. It was published under the news of young Roosevelts death.

Yesterday the child went to lecture to the Americans. It was most unlike most lectures as you can well imagine. But a great success.

Asprey is being very tiresome about my watch but I fear there is nothing to be done. Cest la guerre. But if you pass that way you might prod him with a parasol and say Please Mr Asprey get a move on the Majors watch.

Did you hear the story of Sir Douglas saying to a private soldier " Well my man when did you start the war? "

" Who says I started the war? " answered the man.

your remote,

Scented Kendal Brown.

Head Quarters Independent Force RAF BEF France.
August 15 1918.
Petit Four,

we got back last night after only a few most hectic hours in Paris. I scarcely left the hotel telephone. The Ritz was crammed. I had a room in an attic I couldnt find. It was all a terrific rush. We started back yest morn. On the way we punctured four tyres. I will send back Em Vics in a day or two. I can find it today. It is boiling hot and beautiful. Gold corn fields large shadows. Gleaners a haze of heat a bloom of summer on everything faint noises and tinklings. There has been some news of Conny he was arrested but released again.

What news there is looks better.

yrs Georges Dandin.

August 17 1918.
    Head Quarters Independent Force RAF BEF France.
Dear Cleo (Pâtre not de Merode)
    Thank you for your interesting letter about the bats.
There was only one only Juliet thought that paltry.   I too
dislike bats in a bedroom but not nearly as much as things on
the floor.   A bat never flies down on to your bed be your hair
ever so golden and tangled and silky and luxuriant but mice
rats vipers lizards cobras Karaits centipedes scorpions and lice
crawl into a persons bed.
    From these there is no escape.   A shoe thrown at a bat and
open window will do wonders.   Hillarys appreciation of human
beings is really curious.   It puzzles me.   Somebody wrote to
me the other day and said "The more I see of Hillary the less
I bother about his opinions and the more I like him."   But I
dont think it is so simple as all that.   In one sense his opinions
dont matter but in another sense only his opinions matter take
them away and you take away his essence.   Again in one sense
he is completely ignorant as to the nature of human beings in
another sense he has a sharp nose for the *nature* of people.   In
fact l'etre humain est un paradoxe.
    The third edition of my poems is being printed.   I hate
the publisher.
                    Your most affectionate
                        Barrabas.

Head Quarters Independent Force. RAF BEF France,
        August 19 1918.
Soft Simplicetta,
        Juliet lost a hair not pin but spring yesterday.   It was
found after a long search on the floor.   I have not heard from
you today.
        Madam I hear no word from you today
        My lonely soul implores incessant news,
        What Harmsworth meditates and what the Jews,
        etc
    (Unfinished Sonnet)
                    yours
                        Elijah Fenton.

Head Quarters Independent Force RAF BEF France.
6 September 1918 Battle of the Marne 1914.
Dear Mrs Aphra Behn,
    I wonder if you are wearing a negligé of your favourite
royal purple. See todays Times and whether you are following a
cure to take down your *avoirdupois*. All this is in Mr Davis's
article about the German Empress which will make you rock
with laughter if you read it. He says she always arrived at his
office with a either a lunch box or basket. He adds no German
will go without their second breakfast. Poor innocent as if
that were her second breakfast little does he know that royalties
have a meal wherever they alight during the day. If I were
the Emperor and the Empress I should mind the publications
of these articles almost more than losing Alsace and Lorraine.
If they do lose it. And not that were it not for a war they
never would have been published in their naked sincerity.
There was a loud thunder storm this morning mingled with
hail. It has given me a headache. My thumb is better but
yesterday Wing Commander Landon drove down a wasp on to
my leg and it stung me through the cloth of my breeches Blue
bag was administered but it swelled to an immense size and still
is a little sore. Have you read Les silences du Colonel Bramble
it is a delicious book. Sir Walter Raleigh left last night. Do
you know him? I should like to know what kind of man
Hillary says he is. Possibly a good man. Or possibly something quite impossibly farfetched such a money-seeking man.
                        yrs etc Bully Mutton.

Head Quarters Independent Force,
        RAF. BEF. France.
            September 9.1918.
Carte D'Or,
        the blocks have arrived as you see and I am using the
first sheet and devoting it to a letter to you.
    It is a great comfort to have some nice writing paper once
more. The luncheon with the Italians was great fun. The
child did not go but I went with Col Baldwin. After luncheon
a man played the violin and the tune he payed was called the
Intermezzo out of the Cavalleria Rusticana. You may have

heard of it. He played it in one time and his accompanist played it in another time. Out of which grew an argument. The violinist saying it was it was four time and the accompanist three or vice versa. The argument grew fiercer and the pianist who was a Neapolitan turned white with rage. Someone offered to bet and flung all his money on the table. Then the Neapolitan threatened to go and live somewhere else but all the same was careful in the intensity of his fury not to take the bet.

Finally they became calm and went on playing the tune each in his different way which was satisfactory to everyone except the audience.

After luncheon we were photographed in the pouring rain this took an hour because every time everything was ready I laughed because I could not help it. This made the photographer who was the Neapolitan very angry not with me but with the others who were standing behind me because he said they were trying to make me laugh as indeed they were. Owing to the pouring rain it was impossible to take an instantaneous photograph which every one in vain implored him to do.

Yrs Chateau Pobel.

Head Quarters Independent Force. RAF BEF France.
17 September, 1918.
Plus que Reine,

I am worried to death. But there is no use in going to that. Let us talk of other things.

Have you ever read *Les Dieux ont soif* by Anatole France? I read it when it came out and I am now rereading it. I came across this remark which seems to me to be profound "On n'est jamais assez simplement mise," says one Bint to another.

"Vous dites bien, ma belle," answers the other Bint.

"Mais rien n'est plus couteux en toilette que la simplicité. Et ce n'est pas toujours par mauvais gout que nous mettons des fanfreluches ; c'est quelquefois par économie." This is not only true about Bints clothes it is true about mens clothes about food about art about everything in the world.

Rien n'est plus couteux que la simplicité.
Yrs Chien dent.

Head Quarters Independent Force,
RAF BEF France. 18 September 1918.
Pompeusement Parée,
it is strange that it is much easier to write to someone in
London than it is to write to someone who is in Wales. Sultry
weather continues. I saw General Pershing yesterday. The
child went to see him. And I caught a glimpse of him as we
were going away. In fact he said How do you do Sir to me.
I stumbled and nearly fell down and backed awkwardly out of
the room. You are of course buying your new clothes. I hope
you will not forget your favourite negligé of royal purple. A
new ADC has arrived vice Ravenscroft who is going to be an
SO3. His name is Saumarez. He is in the Scots Guards.
His arm was shot off. He is very nice I think.
                              Yrs Anti-Jacobin.

October 7 1918.
Head Quarters Independent Force, RAF. BEF. France.
Dear Lady Lipton,
We were in Paris yesterday. The day before yesterday in
the Hotel Ritz Sommy arrived after dinner and said there is a
man from the Gaulois who says the Germans have asked for
peace and that the news is going to be published tomorrow.
I said Where is Belloc?
We were expecting him.
Hillary arrived we all went up to the Generals room where
the General and David were. David had been dining with us.
Sommy said.
A man from the Gaulois . . . .
Hillary said Do you know the story of an American who
went to a seance and told it and we laughed.
Sommy said It appears that the Germans . . . .
The General said that reminds me of the story Godfrey
Paine told the Air Board . . . . .
He told it we laughed.
Sommy said they say there is a rumour . . . .
David said have you heard the story of the pilot and . . . .
he told it and we laughed.
Sommy gave it up.   yrs trop fier.

Head Quarters Independent Force.   RAF BEF France.
          October 20.1918.
Reine de Saba,
          thank you very much for the cigarettes which arrived
safely.
          We went to Paris the day before yesterday and came back
yesterday.
          We stayed at the Hotel Ritz.   There I met Madame X——.
She was standing in the passage outside the lift.   Waiting
for the lift was also a Major in the RAF in uniform who in
private life is a professional musician.   We all three got into
the lift.   At that moment before the lift started a Frenchman
walked passed it in uniform and saluted us.   I said to
Madame X—— who is that man?   " A horrible man " she
answered " *a musician* " in clear ringing sharp iciclelike cinglant
accents expressive of infinite contempt.
          The Major looked at her in a way which meant he would
be glad if a crowd of Bolsheviks had rushed at her and torn out
her entrails and waved her insolent head on a pike singing the
Carmagnole.
          I remain yours now and always.
                              Mardrus.

Head Quarters RAF
          Independent Force.   October 21. 1918,
Dear Madame Emile,
          thank you for the letters that I have not received.   We
have had some Japanese gentlemen staying with us.   Conversation with them was not very easy.   They hiss politely when
spoken to.
          At breakfast Sir Walter Lawrence did the civil and asked
them several questions and made several comments on the
weather without getting any response from them.
          At last he said to one of them
          " Is your coffee to your liking? "
          The Japanese thought a little and then said :
          " Its tea."
                              Yours essentially,
                              Hugo Slav.

Head Quarters Independent Force RAF BEF.
11 November 1918.
A HISTORIC DAY.
DEAR COMMANDANT DUFF
I WILL THEREFORE WRITE IN CAPITAL
LETTERS BUT NOT IN RED LETTERS AS THEY ARE
TOO FAINT.
WE RETURNED LAST NIGHT FROM PARIS. WE
HAD BEEN SUMMONED BY MARSHAL FOCH TO
HIS HEAD QUARTERS TEN DAYS BEFORE AND WE
ARRIVED THERE JUST WHEN THE HUN DELE-
GATES WERE EXPECTED. AS YOU KNOW THEY
WERE LATE OWING TO ROAD TROUBLE WE
STAYED AT THE BRITISH MISSION ONE NIGHT
AND THE NEXT DAY WE WENT TO PARIS.
PARIS WAS VERY FULL. IT WAS MOST EXCIT-
ING WITH BITS OF NEWS ARRIVING EVERY
MINUTE. WE GOT THE NEWS OF THE EMPERORS
ABDICATION THE DAY BEFORE YESTERDAY
IN THE AFTERNOON. IN THE NIGHT THERE
WERE MANIFESTATIONS IN THE STREETS. LAST
NIGHT WE GOT THE NEWS OF THE ARMISTICE
AND THE OFFICIAL NEWS THIS MORNING.
YRS PEACEMAKER.

Index